THIS BOOK IS NOT FOR EDISON

Building Business Models for Technology Pioneers

SUNDARA NAGARAJAN

STARDOM BOOKS

www.StardomBooks.com

STARDOM BOOKS

112 Bordeaux Ct.

Coppel, TX 75019, USA

Copyright © 2023 by Sundara Nagarajan

All rights reserved. No part of this book may be reproduced or used in any manner without written permission of the copyright owner except for the use of quotations in a book review. Copyright © 2023 Sundara Nagarajan

FIRST EDITION SEPTEMBER 2023

STARDOM BOOKS, LLC.
112 Bordeaux Ct. Coppel, TX 75019, USA

www.stardombooks.com

Stardom Books, United States
Stardom Alliance, India

The author and publishers have made all reasonable efforts to contact copyright holders for permission and apologize for any omissions or errors in the form of credits given. Corrections may be made to future editions.

THIS BOOK IS NOT FOR EDISON

Sundara Nagarajan

p. 245
cm. 13.5 X 21.5

Category:
BUS025000 - BUSINESS & ECONOMICS / Entrepreneurship
BUS071000 - BUSINESS & ECONOMICS / Leadership

ISBN: 978-1-957456-31-7

DEDICATION

To the countless people who passionately share entrepreneurship knowledge to benefit newcomers to entrepreneurship.

To my mother, my life partner Jyothi, my son Ashok and my extended family of well-wishers.

DISCLAIMER

Technologists and scientists are used to precision. The world of business has many ways. I am a technologist and a disciple of entrepreneurship. This book is based on my learning and insights, that I am sharing with the readers to help them develop perspectives. I do not claim this to be a manual you can use to build your firm. I have tried to put together methods known to work in practical situations. It has several pointers to deeper materials. Take it in the scientific spirit of experimentation and adapt the guidance to your context or discard it if you find it not working. Please expect no guarantees. If you discover any errors or have an alternative perspective, please write to me at
notforedison@innovationscaleup.com

Or visit us at

bit.ly/notforedison

- Sundara Nagarajan

CONTENTS

	Foreword	iii
	Acknowledgments	vii
	Why Did I Write This Book?	ix
	Start Building Your Vehicle	1
1.	Congratulations! You Are Promoted As the CEO!	11
2.	Mind the Gaps	25
3.	Where is Your Customer?	41
4.	Lead with your Purpose and Vision	57
5.	Good Loss and Bad Loss	75
6.	Jump over the Widest Chasm	91
7.	Illuminate Your Firm	109
8.	Manage for Results	125
9.	Grow Yourself and Your Team	141
10.	Raise Capital as a Pro	161
	The Path to Greatness is Rough	181
	APPENDIX 1: Terminology in This Book	191
	APPENDIX 2: Preparing for Investor Interaction	199
	APPENDIX 3: Curated Resources	213
	About The Author	225

A startup is the quickest vehicle to journey from foresight to forecast. If you envision a distant future that you want to create for others and yourself, focus your energies on designing and creating this vehicle that can reliably take you the distance. Smart founders use gravitational slingshot to moonshot their vehicles.

FOREWORD

Many books have been written about entrepreneurship, innovation, and scaling technology-related businesses. But if you are like me, a practitioner involved with startups, whether as a founder, investor, or corporate executive thinking of making a plunge into the world of incubating or starting a disruptive new business and interested in comprehending what it takes to scale businesses, then this book is for you.

Sundara Nagarajan, aka SN, with whom I've shared a nearly four-decade-long acquaintance, skillfully crafts a comprehensive body of work in a meticulously organized narrative. His intention is to aid individuals endeavoring to grasp a panoramic understanding of the intricate issues encompassing the inception, nurturing, and expansion of startups. While the title may insinuate that its content is tailored for those possessing extraordinary business prowess, the reality proves far more encompassing.

Indeed, even individuals like myself, deeply engaged in startup investment as an integral facet of my professional responsibilities, derive immense educational value from this book. Its insights transcend levels of familiarity or expertise in constructing and amplifying business ventures. SN's literary offering is an invaluable resource, extending its benefits to a broad spectrum of readers, regardless of their prior exposure or proficiency in business establishment and growth.

In the dynamic landscape of entrepreneurship, there is a need to weave vision, strategy, execution, and scaling intricately with an understanding of risk-taking and with an eye toward pragmatic realism. Businesses, in general, either scale or perish. Stagnation is indeed a form of perishing. If a business stagnates, one has to conclude that it needs to identify what impedes its progress or has yet to deploy the required tools in a manner that allows it to transcend those challenges.

In this context, SN's approach to this complex topic in this book is a mix of equal parts illustration of strategy and audacity of risk-taking, keys to identifying technological relevance and adaptability of a solution that can be grown into scaled businesses.

Within the pages of this enlightening book, SN takes readers on a voyage through the highs and lows of scaling businesses and the associated challenges. However, what sets this book apart is its focus on equipping the reader with practical tools to conquer the daily obstacles entrepreneurs face. This guidance is provided by an individual who has not only achieved mastery in this realm over several decades of rich career experience but also gained insights from diverse technological roles, including those of an R&D executive, technology manager, startup CEO, and educator.

The true strength of the book lies in its role as a coach. Sn's extensive experience as a gallup coach shines vividly, infusing the content with actionable wisdom. Rather than taking a strictly prescriptive approach, the book's various sections eloquently articulate an array of tools and techniques available to the reader.

For everyone who works with or in startups, be it a founder or an employee, the word "scaling" resonates with both the thrill of possibilities and the overarching shadow of self-doubt, fear, and uncertainty. In the following chapters, SN doesn't shy away from exploring these dualities with a critical view, offering insights from examples and interesting anecdotes that can potentially change the trajectory of any business intending to "scale up."

At the heart of this literary voyage lies a pivotal revelation: scaling isn't a mere extension of growth; it's a holistic orchestration of strategy, innovation, and execution across all facets of a business. SN delves into the world of product design, an essential cornerstone that can either propel a startup forward or become the point of its downfall. The careful balance between technological prowess and a profound understanding of market needs forms the bedrock upon which successful product design stands. He skillfully makes the distinction between product market fit (PMF), product solution fit (PSF), and business model fit (BMF), among other critical elements of a business.

Through vivid anecdotes and expert analysis, SN reminds us that a product isn't just code and features; it embodies market requirements and a fusion of technological brilliance to solve real-world problems. In essence, SN advocates for a symbiotic relationship between innovation and market comprehension, producing solutions that resonate with customers and stakeholders, a philosophy that serves as a central pillar of this invaluable guide.

Turning the pages of this book, the narrative gracefully shifts to one of the most compelling aspects of the startup world—risk. Scaling is a venture immersed in uncertainty, where the calculated dance with risk often becomes a defining moment. Sn elevates this concept to an art form, showcasing how successful scaling hinges on managing risk effectively. As the journey unfolds, readers are educated on the intricacies of risk and presented with a blueprint for managing it. The fusion of vision, innovation, and calculated risk-taking emerges as a recurring theme, cementing SN's wisdom as a beacon for those who dare to challenge the status quo.

He starts modestly in the first chapter, tracing the startup founder's journey, with the aptly named chapter – "congratulations, you are promoted as the CEO." From there, he carefully evolves to highlight the key aspects to pay attention to, such as – the startup's deficiencies, customers, purpose, and vision. He also artfully combines the qualitative aspects, such as strategy, vision purpose, etc., with the quantitative aspects, such as financial metrics and the need to focus on the correct elements of those financial indicators critical for the business. Perhaps his inner coach shines through in subsequent chapters, where he delves into the need to jump over the chasms in any business to tackle the scaling challenges head-on.

His assertion that startups face closure not due to a mere depletion of funds, but more significantly, because of the strategic choices they've made leading to financial exhaustion encapsulates a succinct yet profound summary of his thorough analysis. This viewpoint underscores the essence of his comprehensive examination of the factors influencing the success or failure of startups.

The human element, often the linchpin between mere success and sustainable growth, is dissected with surgical precision. Sn's exploration into team dynamics, professional incentives, emotional resonance, and the nurturing of talent showcases the depth of understanding required to foster an environment where excellence thrives. This section of the book serves as a reminder that a startup's success is a culmination of the commitment, creativity, and camaraderie that its teams bring to the table.

In essence, this book is more than just a guide—it's a manifesto for the modern entrepreneur, a treasure trove of insights crafted by a visionary who has transformed startups through his insightful recommendations and interventions through his current venture, *innovation scaleup advisors,* which is a living entity that practices coaching entrepreneurs with many lessons from this book. Sn's narrative voice resonates with the knowledge and empathy of a coach, offering readers a glimpse into the rollercoaster ride that is scaling. Each lesson in this book is a testament to the resilience required to navigate the labyrinthine startup ecosystem and the audacity to turn challenges into triumphs.

As the final pages are turned, a profound sense of empowerment remains. Sn's words echo as a mentor's guiding voice, encouraging readers to take that audacious step into the unknown, confront challenges with a strategic mindset, and innovate with the unwavering confidence that success is achievable. "***This Book is not for Edison – Building Business Models for Technology Pioneers***" is not just a book—it's a legacy of lessons, a roadmap to scaling greatness, and an invitation to shape the future through innovation, resilience, and strategic brilliance.

Sriram Viswanathan
Founding Managing Partner, Celesta Capital

ACKNOWLEDGMENTS

Throughout my career, I was fortunate to be part of entrepreneurial teams, creating new products. I have learned much from my seniors, customers, partners/team members, peers, and coaches/mentors/trainers. I acknowledge them as a collective, as it will not be practical to name each. I have been reading, listening, and researching entrepreneurship, collecting the pearls of knowledge and wisdom. I applied the principles I learned whenever I got the opportunity and observed what worked and what did not. I have experienced this throughout my life as an entrepreneur and entrepreneurial employee.

I am indebted to many authors and speakers who continue to influence and shape my learning: Alexander Osterwalder, Aswath Damodaran, Ben Lamorte, Brad Feld, Eric Ries, Fred Reichheld, Geoffrey Moore, Jerry Neumann, Jordan Peterson, Justin Wilcox, Kunal Shah, Marc Andreessen, Michael Siebel, Paul Graham, Peter Thiel, Rita G. McGrath, Roger L. Martin, Sam Altman, Shailendra Vyakarnam, Steve Blank, Saras Saraswathi, Uday Phadke, and numerous others I am missing to mention. I have attempted to acknowledge the source of most concepts and allow my readers to go to the original for authentic details.

It is humanly impossible to acknowledge every source of learning. If I have not recognized anyone, it is only my human limitation. I don't claim any part of this book as my original creation, invention, or discovery. I have no claims of originality other than my rendition, and all errors and omissions are mine. I recognize the countless passionate people spreading the knowledge of entrepreneurship, and this book is indebted to them all.

Raam Anand, the founder of Stardom Books, has inspired and coached me to write the first book of my life. I'd like to thank Priyadarshini Mitra, Rekha Krishnaprasad, H.K. Tejas, Ryan Steve

Menezes, and Ranjitha Vijayakumar for being excellent collaborators and contributors to make this book happen. I thank them all from the bottom of my heart.

WHY DID I WRITE THIS BOOK?

Technology is the key to economic growth of nations, cities, and individuals. It is a new capability that triggers change. Technological progress empowers better products and services, manifests in the emergence of new industries, and continuously improves efficiencies. Scientists and technologists pave the way to new products and services through their lifelong dedication to research and industrial product development. Only a few technologists succeed as founders and build economically valuable firms. However, inventive technologists most often do not become wealthy. Most of us need to gain the know-how to start with an innovative idea and execute our startup ventures successfully.

Let's look closely at the legendary founders from the times of the industrial revolution. We will notice more diversity than similarities. And it is the differences that defined them and led to their success. All too often, we are oblivious to something critical to our success—our personality, our natural traits—what we do well naturally most of the time, without even thinking about it. Entrepreneurship is a kind of leadership that develops on top of our natural traits by mastering ourselves and adding the knowledge and skills to enhance our competence.

So, I passionately help technologists to scale up their innovation and generate economic value to impact our society positively. This book is an effort to share the state-of-the-art practices I have learned as a technologist and product developer. I aim to help you, the technologist, scale up your innovation as a thriving firm. When a few of you acknowledge that this book had a role in your success, I will consider it to have served my purpose. I have not discussed how to research, problem-solve, innovate, or build unique systems—I know that is not where we technologists fall short.

This book is irrelevant to you if you are talented and possess exceptional business acumen like Edison. On the other hand, if you feel a gap in developing your perspective as a founder, or an aspiring founder, this book is for you!

I wish you success and fulfilment.

Sundara Nagarajan
Bangalore, India.

START BUILDING YOUR VEHICLE

"Your time is limited, so don't waste it living someone else's life. Don't be trapped by dogma – which is living with the results of other people's thinking. Don't let the noise of others' opinions drown out your own inner voice. And most important, have the courage to follow your heart and intuition. They somehow already know what you truly want to become. Everything else is secondary."
— Steve Jobs.

A startup is the quickest vehicle to journey from foresight to forecast. If you envision a distant future that you want to create for others and yourself, focus your energies on designing and creating this vehicle that can reliably take you the distance. Smart founders use gravitational slingshot to moonshot their vehicle.

EVERYTHING BEGINS WITH A TECHNOLOGICAL REVOLUTION

A *technological revolution* starts when many innovations arrange as *components* to form a *new technological system* that will profoundly impact the economy, society, and political order (1). It feels like a wave that changes everything on its way. Perhaps, managing and controlling fire is among the earliest technologies humans developed. The last decades of 1800 saw inventions based on electromagnetism from Tesla, Edison, Bell, and numerous others. 1950 marked the beginning of digital computing and artificial intelligence. The decade of 1990 saw the *convergence* of computer technology, data networking, and consumer electronics. In the decade of 2000, we witnessed the culmination of artificial intelligence, cloud computing, and mobile communication. We live through the advances in generative AI, blockchain, extended reality, quantum computing, 3D printing, etc., that will transform how we live, interact, work, and entertain. It is plausible to foresee *virtual immortalization* in AI-powered digital twins—after a human is gone physically or even when alive, the digital twin could continue to talk and learn "like him or her" and continue contributing. All technologies augment our natural capabilities, it is the cusp of the human brain to be augmented like never before.

Technological revolution brings new capabilities that open new possibilities for value creation through an explosive sprout of firms supported by financial capital, sometimes termed a *bubble* after the fact. The phase that follows experiences, the systematic adoption of new technologies, and a new order comes into existence, only to be disrupted by the next technological revolution. The instances mentioned above are micro-revolutions. Carlota Perez identifies five technological revolutions in two hundred years that profoundly impacted society (2), the fifth being the Information revolution that started in the 1970s.

THIS BOOK IS FOR PRODUCT BUILDERS

Thank you for choosing this book from a million choices and allocating your time to start reading it. This book aims to help technologists, scientists, and functional specialists to become better entrepreneurs. As first-time entrepreneurs, these professionals need help reducing risk while building a thriving firm based on innovative ideas. This book is meant for *product entrepreneurs*. This book uses the word "product" to include "services" delivered for a transactional fee or *outcome-as-a-service* (e.g., software-as-a-service, lighting-as-a-service, etc.). The *service economy* is well-established, wherein customers consume benefits and pay for what they consume. The dichotomy between product and service is now replaced with the product-service continuum (3). In this book, service refers to products delivered for transactional consumption. It is important to remember the distinction with business models of the service sector, such as *consulting, professional/engineering services*, manufacturing services, distribution, and *outsourcing* which essentially augments people and other resources for the client firm.

SCIENTISTS, TECHNOLOGISTS, AND ENGINEERS

In the context of this book, the word *technologist* stands for engineers, software professionals, scientists, and other professional experts who have limited to no experience or education in trading, commerce, or business management. This book focuses on the context of digital business:

- Firms that advance or *invent* digital technologies (computer science, artificial intelligence, data networks, extended reality, and so on)—**DeepTech**.
- Firms that *deploy* components of digital technologies combined with advances in various other technology domains to create new experiences for people—**DigitalTech**.

The author's life and work have been in this domain; therefore, this book is most relevant to readers from that domain attempting to build their ventures. Readers from other disciplines might also find this book relevant and valuable, but the author does not claim applicability beyond the digital technology domain.

WHO IS THE *FOUNDER*?

The founder is the primary entrepreneur accountable for the new firm's impactful, vital decisions and strategy. *Intrapreneur* is an employee of a mature enterprise with the vision for a new business initiative or appointed by the management to lead a new business unit. In the context of this book, the *founder* is the startup CEO of a new technology business venture, and the word represents entrepreneur, intrapreneur, and co-founder.

The co-founder is a management team member working under the leadership of the founder. Co-founders are usually functional leaders who support realizing the founder's vision. Even when two or more leaders come together to establish a venture with an "equal" partnership, one is selected or elected as the leader to make the ultimate business decisions and lead the vision and strategy. If an organization lacks clarity regarding startup CEO role, differences among the founding team members will be an eventuality. Developing an agreement and an articulated understanding among the team members founding a venture is essential to building firms that can scale.

IS IT NATURE OR NURTURE?

Just as leadership is both nature and nurture, entrepreneurship (or, *entrepreneurial leadership*) is also nature and nurture. The body of work on positive psychology and strengths-based development is based on three assumptions. The following is an extract from Gallup's Strengths-based Development principles (4).

- Only some behaviors can be learned. Many behaviors that lead to excellence are nearly impossible to acquire. Natural talent matters. The skills you practice, or gain knowledge can only augment your natural talents.
- The best in a role delivers the same outcomes using different behaviors. The best play to their natural talents,

performing the activity in a way that works for them. The result, not the way you achieve it, defines greatness.
- Weakness fixing prevents failure; strengths building leads to success. If we build on our strengths and develop the things we naturally do well, those efforts are more likely to lead to success.

Gallup promotes two assessment models—Clifton Strengths (5) and Builder Profile 10 (6). Dr. Jordan B. Peterson has developed assessment tools for another model known as the Big Five or OCEAN (7) assessment (8). These assessments support you in exploring your talents and unleashing your potential to be the best you can be. It is essential to get the help of a qualified coach to support your development when using these assessment tools. *Self-awareness* and *Others-awareness* (differences are advantageous, people need one another) are essential skills for successful leaders, especially founders. This book does not delve into the personality traits and development of founders. This book avoids quoting the behaviors of successful entrepreneurs like Elon Musk, who is naturally exceptionally talented (9).

While experts differ on whether 98% fail or 70% fail, or numbers in between, there is no disagreement with the fact that most startups fail. One of the crucial reasons most startups fail is the *lack of a founder's preparedness*. The outcome would be disappointing if one decides to climb Mount Everest and sets out to climb on a good day equipped with some random information. There is a near 100% probability of failure to climb to the top or even a severe threat to life. The situation with entrepreneurship is no different. In the past, only those individuals with innate talents and personality traits could succeed in building lasting firms. Many successful entrepreneurs came from business or trading families. History records and celebrates successful entrepreneurs from centuries ago. However, until recently, very little organized help was available to seeking entrepreneurs to build their ventures. Founders must seek help from one or more coaches and mentors to support their journey and *the climb* to their pinnacle of success.

THIS IS THE BEST TIME TO BE A FOUNDER

The world order is slowly but surely shifting towards democratic capitalism—a free market economic system with an emphasis on the private enterprise. Undoubtedly, now is the best time to be an entrepreneur, and the times are only going to get better—more and more help is available for aspiring entrepreneurs through education, incubation, and financial support to build their ventures. There is an increasing shift towards *entrepreneurial universities* (10) worldwide, and entrepreneurship education is introduced at the secondary school level. The subject matter of entrepreneurship is now maturing to become learnable and trainable. On coursera.org, there are close to 3,000 online courses on entrepreneurship and startup. It would be wise for anyone to either start or run a startup taking the benefit of experience being shared freely on the internet.

While common sense and straightforward principles are essential for all successful practices, handling complexity effectively requires relevant, more profound knowledge. Nurturing needs the systematic creation of the body of knowledge through research. There is an enormous body of foundational research and practitioner stories on entrepreneurship—far too much for any startup founder or student to read and internalize.

This book attempts to distil and compile relevant guidance for the first-time technologist founder who aspires to build an impactful firm at scale. It aims to open the founder's mind to critical aspects and pointers for creating a firm. By no means is this book a complete manual or playbook. This book points to different methods, tools, and frameworks. But it does not describe, propose, or promote any specific approach. The intent is to create awareness for the founders to explore themselves in depth.

WHO IS THIS BOOK FOR?

This book is written for:

- First-time founders (or aspiring founders, co-founders) of technology-enabled firms with deep knowledge and experience in the technology domain.
- Researchers, Scientists, R&D engineers, and students from the technology domain who aspire to turn their ideas and inventions into commercially viable products or services.
- Employees of established companies who lead internal initiatives to create new technology products or services (or *intrapreneurs*.)
- Leaders of digital transformation of their business.
- Technology and technology-based small and medium enterprise (SME) leaders experiencing stagnation in their business and exploring new ideas to grow economic value through diversification or transformation.
- Professionals in technology business incubators and accelerators, mentors, strategy consultants, and coaches who support and advise technology startup entrepreneurs.

HOW TO USE THIS BOOK?

Some readers may want to read the book starting from Chapter 1 and continuously read it to the back cover if their interest sustains. However, I don't expect or recommend that approach amid a busy startup founder's life. You can go directly to the Chapter that relates to where your firm is in the journey, understand the concepts as deeply as possible, and try to *practice them in your firm*. You will find key takeaways at the end of every chapter, synthesizing what the chapter presents.

The book's chapters are sequenced as closely as possible to the journey of learning for a founder. The footnotes acknowledge the source of information or insight quoted, and serve as deeper references on the topic that readers may consider reading to develop depth on that micro topic.

The journey of an idea to a *thriving state,* as identified in the framework presented in the book, would take seven to fifteen years for a DeepTech firm. Considering the speed at which knowledge is expanding today, it is indeed a long time. Please visit the companion website for the book ***bit.ly/notforedison*** for errata, additional information, and, most importantly, to provide your feedback to improve the usefulness of this book.

z<F<z<e 2<~#

1. Carlota Perez, "Technological Revolutions and Financial Capital: The Dynamics of Bubbles and Golden Ages," Edward Elgan Publishing Limited, 2022, ISBN 1-84064-922-4, Amazon Kindle Edition, pp. 27-51. Readers interested in developing perspectives on the nature of macro technological trends and how they trigger significant step changes in society must read this book.
2. Ibid.
3. Service Economy, Wikipedia, URL: https://en.wikipedia.org/wiki/Service_economy: Last accessed 01-Sep-2022.
4. Gallup Clifton Strengths, URL: https://www.gallup.com/cliftonstrengths/en/home.aspx: Last accessed 01-Sep-2022.
5. Tom Rath and Barry Conchie, "Strengths-based Leadership: Great Leaders, Teams, and Why People Follow," Gallup Press, 2008, ISBN 978-1-59562-025-5.
6. Jim Clifton and Sangeeta Badal, "Born to Build: How to Build a Thriving Startup, A Winning Team, New Customers, and Your Best Life Imaginable," Gallup Press, 2008, ISBN 978-1-59562-127-6.
7. OCEAN stands for Openness to Experience, Conscientiousness, Extraversion, Agreeableness, and Neuroticism—the Big Five dimensions, as they are referred to.
8. URL: https://www.understandmyself.com/personality-assessment: Last accessed 01-Sep-2022.
9. If you are interested in biographies, you will enjoy reading Ashlee Vance's "Elon Musk: How the Billionaire CEO of SpaceX and Tesla is Shaping Our Future," Penguin Random House UK, 2015, ISBN: 978-0-753-55563-7.
10. Simone Boruck Klein and Frederico Cesar Mafra Pereira, "Entrepreneurial University: Conceptions and Evolution of

Theoretical Models," 2020, URL: https://doi.org/10.12712/rpca.v14i4.43186

1

CONGRATULATIONS!

YOU ARE PROMOTED AS THE CEO

"We have a brilliant engineer or technologist or somebody with a business model insight that's unique and different. They usually are fairly unidimensional, rarely have they managed people or run marketing, or been a CFO. So, entrepreneurs really need help in directions that they're not familiar with themselves, where their background isn't. They usually fail not because of what they are strong at but what they might be weak at."

– *Vinod Khosla,* (1) *Entrepreneur and Venture Capitalist.*

WHERE ARE YOU COMING FROM?

Naren was born in a remote village in India, where his father was a schoolteacher. After completing his education in his mother tongue medium, he was selected to a premier engineering school. He was hardworking, he did well and joined the industry. Naren just crossed forty years and is flying high as a corporate leader and head of a product engineering unit. He connected the dots very well. His managers chose him whenever a situation was ambiguous and required quick decision-making involving multiple disciplines. He has been the one to spot any new technology trend in his domain and imagine how that trend would change the world. He built and grew high-performing teams as a middle-level manager. His managers named him a high potential and opened developmental opportunities for him. Everyone felt he had consolidated well in his corporate career in the global technology company. Naren had never imagined he would start a business. His manager could not hold his surprise when Naren told him that he wanted to quit the job to start a company— *"Are you sure?"* Of course. Naren's passion, intuition, and self-assurance propelled his decision— a foresight of the new world order waiting to emerge and a calling he couldn't resist. And here he is, leaving a steady job, assembling a few other professionals, and envisioning building a globally impacting DeepTech venture!

You may be like Naren, a successful corporate employee, technologist, or functional expert, leaving a prosperous corporate career and venturing to build a technology company inspired by an inner calling others can't understand. Or, you may not be so successful in a corporate job, finding your employment constraining or boring. But you have several ideas that might lead to a profitable technology venture. You could be one of those unlucky employees impacted by corporate restructuring who couldn't find an equivalent job soon. You may also be the lucky employee of a "unicorn" startup who became wealthy early in life beyond your imagination. Or you may be a scientist or academic researcher experienced in a world-class research lab. Or you are someone who always cherished the dream of "being on your own" after getting some industry experience. Naren represents you all, the first-time entrepreneur coming out of employment to start a venture.

Asim was lucky to be born into a respected business family. His father founded a business that became a mature listed company. Asim had the opportunity to grow up listening to his father's business. His father had successfully built and ran an agricultural economy firm in a small town, giving Asim a comfortable early life growing up, watching his father's pleasures of building the business. Asim did not get to see his father's small daily pains. But occasionally, the family experienced a few turbulent times but soon came out. Asim's parents supported him in getting educated in the best accessible universities in the world, studying engineering and business management courses. As Asim grew up, his father occasionally involved him in small business tasks. Later, Asim joined the traditional family business full-time, which had started to show signs of decline. He inherited the values and capital from his father's business. Asim decided to diversify into a new venture in the emerging technology industry that shows the potential to scale up several times. Asim represents the generations of children from traditional family businesses now venturing for the first time into the unfamiliar territory of emerging technology ventures.

Mary has been a curious and diligent science student. She had tinkered with electronics and software since she was in middle school. Her classmates thought she would become a scientist. She scored high in science subjects, got admission into the best engineering schools, and became a gold medal-winning Ph.D. Her research work and findings indicated potential to be applied in the industrial context. She did not want to pursue an academic career or corporate employment. Instead, she decided to start a business. You may not be like Mary, but you are a student who is impatient to complete school and earn degrees but wants to build a product business. Mary represents you all, the student entrepreneurs.

Your motivation may be the wealth you would create, the power you get to enjoy, or merely the positive impact on society that you sincerely care about. The desire to create appears to be dormant in every human being seeking the right environment and opportunity—like the seed waiting for moisture. People take the plunge when their intuition paints a compelling future vision that appears plausible to them.

It is common knowledge that most entrepreneurial ventures fail, and the entrepreneur may lose the opportunity, money, reputation, and respect in the community. Still, entrepreneurship is only on the rise. The primary reason is the possibility of disproportionate success for the few individuals who succeed and their impact on the world—society's overall economic advancement results from entrepreneurial ventures, whether successful or not. Consequently, there is ever-improving ecosystem support for aspiring entrepreneurs, cyclic in nature, however. Most importantly, more risk capital is available to support promising business ideas. There is more acceptance of entrepreneurship in society today than ever before.

But is entrepreneurship right for an engineer, scientist, or functional specialist such as an accountant or doctor? Should you be the company's principal *founder* or an entrepreneurial employee, nicely termed a *co-founder*? Do you need industry experience or family wealth to start a business? The indications are that it doesn't matter. What kind of a venture should you attempt? When should you decide to venture out full-time to start a company? Before you venture out, how much of a personal safety net should you have? Finding answers to these and several other fundamental questions is best before starting a firm. Often the answers are personal and unique to you.

WHEN YOU STARTUP, YOU ARE SIGNING UP TO BE THE CEO

Let us proceed if you have decided to venture out or are already operating such a venture. Congratulations! You have promoted yourself to be the CEO, the pinnacle of the management ladder of any business or institution. The only next step to grow from this level is to manage larger and larger enterprises—ideally, your venture or another established company. Wow! But are you ready for the job? Most established companies groom top potential employees to become CEOs over many years. One gets the top job, and possibly the others get the CEO/CXO positions in other enterprises. *The hardest job in management is the "first-time CEO."* (2) In this book, we shall refer to this role as the *founder*, inspired by the idea of building an institution.

Now, if you are a *co-founder* accountable for a functional area, you are the CXO. The challenges are like being a business leader with a functional area of ownership. While the CEO is like the captain of a team, CXO is a player who must contribute their part to make the venture successful. The good news is that you could grow incrementally, at a pace slightly faster than your venture's growth. Or you could be wise to hire appropriate professionals as employees to perform critical leadership roles in the business. Remember, you are building a business model and executing it.

Growing yourself is a careful combination of developing your competence to manage yourself, your team, and the business. You must expand your leadership and business knowledge ahead of your business growth, and scaling up yourself precedes scaling up your business. You may choose not to continue as your venture's CEO as it grows and seek to appoint a professional CEO to scale it up further as a larger company.

WHAT TYPE OF AN ENTREPRENEUR ARE YOU?

Ryan Levesque classifies people who start a business into four types, (3) and each has its pitfalls to watch out for. Out of these, if you are an undecided entrepreneur, it is better to start a business to develop the capability to build and run a business. That is a transferrable skill, and you can grow and scale your business and possibly move to be one of the other three types of entrepreneurs.

Entrepreneurial Type	Motivational Characteristics	Pitfalls: What to watch out for?
Mission-based	Pursue a specific mission and make a positive impact	Tend to struggle with making money and can finally fail to create the impact they set out to do.
Passion-based	Something you love, and you are excited to share it with the world	Becoming dispassionate about what you started with and losing the excitement of their passion.
Opportunity-based	See the potential in an unsatisfied demand and motivated by growth	Start wondering about the purpose of what they do and develop an identity crisis.
Undecided	Know you want a business but are unsure of what it is, or circumstances force them to start independently.	Not sticking to anything long enough to build something substantial.

CASH IS THE WEDGE THAT HOLDS YOUR BOULDER

Imagine building your business as rolling a heavy boulder up the slope. The boulder is the *business system* you build—people, culture, processes, tools, etc. that deliver economic value. The business system implements your business model. At any point, the height of the boulder from the ground is the net economic value.

THIS BOOK IS NOT FOR EDISON

The business's cash position is the wedge that helps you retain the boulder in position and prevents you from slipping down. The cash position combines the capital and *profits retained* in the business. When you receive an external capital infusion, you get your wedge bigger, but it does not raise the boulder up or reduce your effort to move it up. It just helps you to hold the boulder from slipping down. Capital helps speed up the adoption of a relevant idea. This is an essential factor to consider in the fast-changing technology domains. Therefore, founders must make a careful trade-off between external capital and profits reinvested to scale up the firm for the growth they aspire.

Consider this trade-off in building a highly differentiated perfume, whose formula is managed as a trade secret among the founder and a couple of close associates. Being highly differentiated, the *gross margin* when selling the product can be high. That provides enough money systematically grow the brand over several years by expanding distribution and production. Significant capital may not be essential to scale such a business. On the other hand, if this business could raise a lot of external capital, it could reach the pinnacle of market adoption sooner.

CB Insights found that 70% of upstart tech companies fail — usually around 20 months after first raising financing (with about $1.3M in total funding closed.) They publish regular startup failure post-mortem reports analyzing failed startups in the spirit of learning (4). CB Insights also publishes its analysis regularly on specific reasons for failure (5). The top reason for the failure of technology-based ventures is "Ran out of cash/failed to raise capital." These are two are different situations but may be closely linked. Running out of cash is a result or *outcome*, not a cause.

Conserving and optimizing the available capital, or *capital optimization* is a critical capability the founder/CEO must have. Using the available capital, the founder must establish evidence for economic value creation and communicate it effectively to investors to raise additional capital. Raising capital and capital allocation are critical competencies the founder must develop to make their ideas and dreams a reality.

SUCCESSFUL STARTUPS AVOID CATASTROPHIC FAILURES

A firm must shut down when it runs out of cash. Successful founders steer their firms to a position to keep the customers with the business and to earn enough customer revenue to pay market-competitive compensation to all the employees. They detect and avoid failure modes to keep their firms changing and adapting continuously. Founders achieve this state by optimizing the capital needed to support their *search for a sustainable business model*. This doesn't mean the firm will scale up to become a large enterprise. Numerous micro, small, and medium enterprises (MSMEs) thrive and generate significant employment in most countries. When the firm *thrives*, the founder has the option and opportunity to build a scalable firm or remain small as a *lifestyle business*.

Developing and scaling a firm is a *multi-dimensional challenge*. Failing to manage the numerous dimensions will result in the firm's demise. Most technologists and engineers are deeply anchored in the physical sciences domain: physics, chemistry, biology, computer science, etc. A firm's successful management is influenced more by social sciences: economics, political science, psychology, sociology, etc. Technician founders with a natural flair for social sciences are at ease building firms that grow.

Learning to do business has many similarities with the game of chess. It does not take long to understand the basic rules of chess, possibly an hour for a novice. The game presents a large number of possibilities for moves (6). While a chess game is exciting to analyze after the game is completed, playing and winning while being in the game is hard. Analyzing older games (developing "best practices") is an excellent way to learn certain game patterns in strategic thinking.

Enterprise building also has similarities with the games of soccer or cricket. There is a limited time window of opportunity to play a game. There are rules that govern the game, but the ground conditions, weather and player's effectiveness, etc. influence the game's outcome. The teams must continuously monitor, innovate and respond to emerging, unpredictable situations. This makes the process complex and unsuitable to apply "best practices" watching others play, most of the time.

And finally, venturing to create a firm is also like playing tennis. The player who scores the last game point wins. We have seen world champions reaching the match point with the opponent having the advantage and recovering from there to win the title. Resilient survival is essential to win the game, ultimately.

SOMETIMES, IT MAY BE WISE TO BE THE CO-FOUNDER

Successful entrepreneurship requires the founder to grow from an expert in a function (e.g., research or engineering) to a generalist manager. Statistically speaking, being a co-founder is more likely to create ultra-high wealth for you than any other means, including being a founder! For every successful, visible founder who creates massive wealth, a few less visible co-founders create an excellent quantum of wealth for themselves at a lower risk. Such wealth creation is unlikely even for a successful employee in a profitable multinational corporation. You must carefully consider being a founder versus a co-founder in a startup if you are a scientist/technologist, engineer, or functional expert par excellence.

Being a co-founder means you have substantial stock compensation or a stake in the firm. Typically, a co-founder owns 10% or higher shareholding among the pool of equity the founder and other key leaders of the firm own together, excluding the equity held by investors in the firm's early stage. Being a co-founder also comes with significant responsibilities beyond your functional expertise area. Understanding the fundamental principles of entrepreneurship and applying them in the context of the firm aligned with the founder is essential to be an effective CXO, and the contents of this book are as relevant to co-founders as much as it is to the founders. Cofounders must trust and accept the leadership of the founder.

YOU MUST FIT WITH THE MARKET WELL

The fit between the founder and the market is the most important early indicator of the success of an idea growing as a thriving firm. This *founder-market fit* (FMF) is not just about the industry experience or expertise of the founder. Every successful innovative startup firm is transformative. Too much experience might limit your disruption potential. Of course, the optimum experience level varies with the industry—for instance, a consumer experience solution versus a medical equipment. The founder must have a healthy obsession with the idea and an authentic empathy (and love) for the customers of the idea. The founder's personal values, personality, and behavior profile should be compatible with the practices of that industrial domain— starting from how one dresses or communicates. Customers and investors keenly watch the founder, especially in the early stages of the firm. It is hard to fully determine this fit until the founder actively engages with the customers and the ecosystem.

You can sense FMF as you resonate with customers and other people and gain their support for your solution—from your customers and influencers on adopting the product. FMF is your first competitive advantage. (7) (8) FMF answers this crucial question: *"Why this founder (and the leadership team) is best suited to succeed in monetizing this market opportunity?"* Many investors consider FMF a better indicator of success for startups. So, watch out for the resonance.

From the CB Insights analysis referred to above, the top reasons for startup failure are *no market need* (solution looking for a customer's problem,) *getting outcompeted*, and a *flawed business model*. We will primarily address these three reasons in the following five chapters.

Let's begin the journey!

KEY TKEAWAYS AND ACTION PLANNING

1. Choosing to be the founder of a venture, you are choosing to be the CEO to build a firm, not only a product, a feature, or a

technology.
2. A profound purpose must drive you to persist through the strains of venture creation. Only when the purpose is deep does grit is sustainable.
3. You must carefully choose between being the founder/startup CEO, an entrepreneurial employee (co-founder), a salaried entrepreneur (or intrapreneur), or an inventor/technologist.
4. We must understand and love the people we want to serve—our beneficiaries and customers--for profit or otherwise.
5. A deep purpose must drive you to persist through the stress and strains of venture creation. Only when the purpose is deep does grit is sustainable.

CALL TO ACTION

Write the following as a document. If you have co-founders, do this exercise collectively around the idea of your startup firm.
1. Why are you starting this startup? Or why are you joining this startup? What success would look like for you?
2. Who is your customer, and how do you want to serve your customer?
3. What do you want to create for the customer (product or service)?
4. What do you want to achieve for yourself? Answer this question in *one sentence* in *your* terms. Your customers may want something else. You will adapt your offering to achieve the firm's and your goals. Don't hesitate to specify this in monetary terms. Make it quantifiable so you know you achieved it and your emotion toward it. For example, the statement can be any *one* of the following. I will feel *confident* if I can build a thriving firm of hundreds of employees. I will feel *successful* if I can make a personal wealth of 1M USD in five years. I will be happy if I help ten customers overcome their challenge in five years (the social impact you want to create.) Avoid stating it negatively; for example, I will feel

disappointed...

5. What are your constraints and guiding principles? For example, I will invest at most 10,000 USD in the firm. Or I will not borrow. Or I will (not) raise venture capital to scale up my firm.

6. Write your firm's "future history" describing how you envision the change in as much detail as possible. Write about your firm in the past tense as it has happened. For instance: "NewCo has saved over 100,000 lives with its early warning device for heart attack, establishing a negative trend in death due to heart disease. The company closed the year with thriving, achieving a RoCE of 25%."

Do the above reflection as a primary founder and share it with your co-founders before they make their sentences so that you can explore the alignment more easily. Reflect on this in as detail as you can. For instance, when you say you will be happy serving ten customers, should you do that profitably, or are you willing to do it voluntarily or accept some loss? Would your constraints and guiding principles conflict with your ability to execute your plan? Capturing the emotion (feeling) is as important as the quantitative goals.

REFERENCES

Quote: Harry Stebbings podcast: The Twenty Minute VC with Vinod Khosla, Feb 24, 2020.

1. https://avc.com/2004/01/you_are_only_a_-2/ Fred Wilson: You are only a first-time CEO once (2004), accessed on 20-Jan-2022.
2. Ryan Levesque, "Choose. The Single Most Important Decision Before Starting Your Business," Hay House, 2019, Amazon Kindle Edition, pp.24.
3. https://www.cbinsights.com/research/startup-failure-post-mortem/ accessed on 20-Jul-2022.
4. https://www.cbinsights.com/research/startup-failure-reasons-top/ accessed on 20-Jul-2022
5. How many possible move combinations are there in chess? http://www.bernmedical.com/blog/how-many-possible-move-combinations-are-there-in-chess accessed on 20-Jan-2022.
6. Jillian Canning, "The Importance of Founder-Market Fit & How to Highlight It While Fundraising," Forbes, January 15, 2020, URL: https://www.forbes.com/sites/jilliancanning/2020/01/15/the-importance-of-founder-market-fit--how-to-highlight-it-while-fundraising: Last accessed 01-Sep-2022.
7. Adith Podhar, "How to assess Founder Market Fit — A framework," August 6, 2020, URL: https://adithpodhar.medium.com/how-to-assess-founder-market-fit-a-framework-3219607ef833: Last accessed 01-Sep-2022.

2

MIND THE GAPS

Everybody has a plan until they get punched in the mouth.

– *Mike Tyson* (1)

I HAVE A GREAT IDEA~

GIVE ME YOUR MONEY...

Naren is sitting in front of me, frustrated and nervous. He had started his firm, leaving a successful career in an MNC with deep technology insight and ideas. He had outstanding credentials in the technology industry to his credit. A few high net worth (HNI) individuals were ready to support him with early funding to build his product idea. With some money in hand, he got started building the product. Startup magazines and newsletters interviewed him. He was invited to deliver talks and be part of panels at emerging technology conferences and startup events. His technology implementation is coming along nicely, and he started sharing the concept with people in his circle. There was interest from multiple industry sectors—real estate, hospitals, educational institutions, etc. Many of them had good things to say. Whenever he met with professionals from the venture capital firms in the events in which he participated, they had encouraging words to say. He and his startup appeared to be on a roll.

In his previous employment, Naren's co-founder John, VP-Sales, was a star sales leader. He signed up a few channel partners on commission. But only a couple of prospective customers were willing to engage with the prototype. Only one was willing to try, but it required significant unanticipated work to implement features for that customer prospect. The progress was slower than expected because he did not have enough technical people on his team. The star VP-Sales returned to tell Naren what the product and collaterals lacked. Naren believed that his product must develop more for customers to see its full capabilities. How could there be customer revenue when the product is not yet fully ready to be sold and supported? There were many meetings but no meaningful follow-up. He thought he needed some more funding to build the product faster.

When Naren approached the venture capitalists for investment, they wanted to see more "traction." Why is no one willing to support his technological breakthrough idea? Despite the industry experience, research, and plan, he appears to be slipping. Money in the company fast ran out, and there was no new investor interest. Existing HNI investors are unwilling to invest more, even though they are supportive and patient (what else could they do?) He started dipping into his savings to keep the product development going. Every prospective investor or professional well-wisher he met had several questions and ideas to offer. But no investor seems to be in a hurry. He followed through with those discussions sincerely, but there was no offer to invest in his firm. Naren was uneasy that the venture capitalists "did not get it" despite his detailed explanations of the potential of his technology. He wants help to raise equity funding from venture capitalists.

This is the typical scenario with many technologist entrepreneurs, professionals from R&D Labs, academic research, etc. The number one external help founders seek is to raise equity funding without internalizing what investors are looking for. "Ran out of cash or failed to raise new capital" is the number one reason CB Insights (2), has discovered for startup failure. Why do most technologists-led ventures land in this situation?

JOURNEY THROUGH THE INNOVATION LIFECYCLE CURVE

Schumpeter (1942) (3), Joe M. Bohlen & George M. Beal (1957) (4), Rogers (1962), Frank M. Bass (1969) (5), Geoffrey Moore (1991) (6) and Uday Phadke, Shailendra Vyakarnam & Sam Dods (2017) (7) have studied the nature of innovation diffusion and the presence of discontinuities in the journey of an innovative idea (a new solution to a significant problem) from its origination to broad adoption. People adopting a new idea, even with apparent advantages, is difficult. According to Rogers (8), innovations require a lengthy period of many years from the time when they become available to the time when they are adopted. Rogers's theory of *diffusion of innovations* explains the why, the what, and how innovations get adoption. He also introduces categorizing people based on their participation in the adoption process as *innovators, early adopters, early majority, late majority, and laggards* (9). The nature of the journey of a firm from its conception to maturity and market leadership follows an S-shaped adoption curve, as shown in the figure. The focus of this book is on the early stages of innovation adoption. So, we are concerned mainly with the innovators, early adopters, and part of the early majority that constitutes about 33% of the total population of adopters (customers.) A product winning about one-third of the estimated maximum number of customers is a strong indicator of **Product-Market Fit (PMF).**

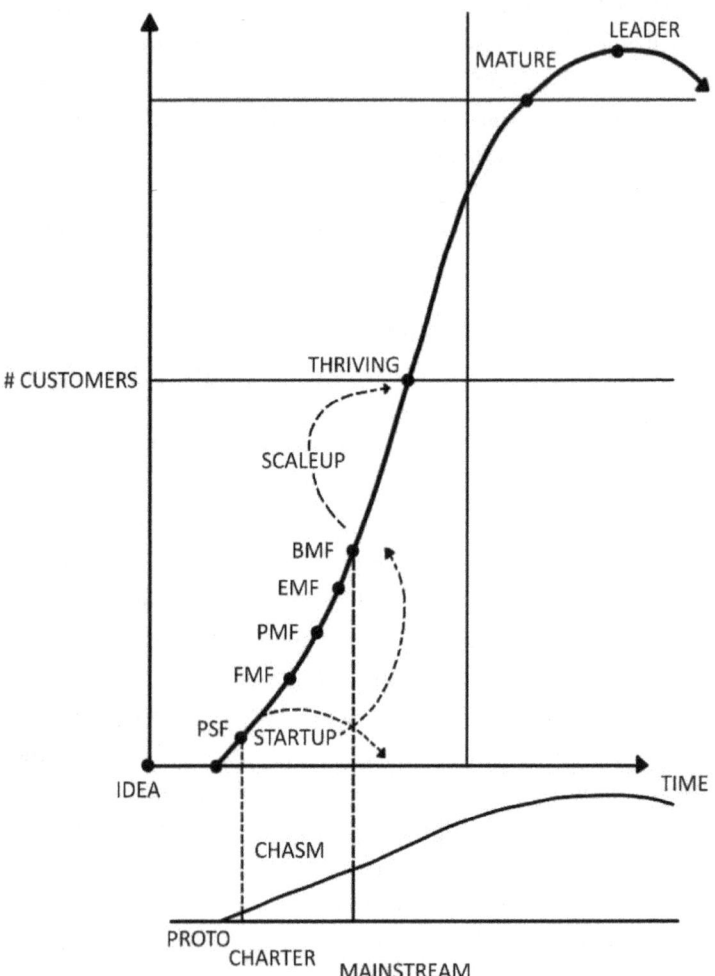

Everything starts with creativity and imagination to create an **invention** or an *idea*. Often this process is intuitive, based on the inventor's observation, knowledge, experiences, and creativity. Scientific research results in inventions that must be proven feasible for practical applications. This phase of work is broadly known as *technology development*, and it happens in a research setting. Following the technology development phase, which typically ends with the lab demonstration, it can enter the *product development* phase, when the technology is matched with a real-world problem it can solve. The transition of the technological breakthrough to a product idea (or *solution*) is a cognitive process in a creative mind that develops a *foresight*. A bunch of assumptions supports this foresight.

The invention or idea happens before the curve's origin, $t = 0$. It does not become an **innovation** until people can use it in the real world and pay for it. Innovation is the origin of this curve, the *business idea*—the 0th milestone in *possibly* building a firm. It is a solution that may fulfill a need for someone or solve a problem someone suffers. It represents the point when the founder has an innovative thought and concept that may be used for **financial gain**. Solving hard problems in society and improving people's lives without any direct financial benefit inspires many founders. Even with such altruistic goals for *non-profit*, the firm that solves the problem must have an economic model that sustains and grows the firm to create the **impact** the founder envisions.

This curve shows the growth in the number of customers (adopters) as time advances. The highest point on the curve is the maximum cumulative number of active customers the product (firm) achieves.

According to Rogers, the adoption of any innovation grows slowly in the initial period with innovators and early adopter category of customers, who form about 16% of the total customers for the new product. Only when the *early majority* of customers or the mainstream customers accept the innovation does the innovation become commercially viable. Most innovations fail to add customers, resulting in the firm dying. This gap between the idea and its adoption is characterized as the *chasm* or *valley of innovation death (VOID).*

Founders must have a reasonable estimate of the chasm they would face as they build their firm. The size of the chasm indicates the capital needed to build the firm and the associated risk. The two critical parameters to size the chasm are the width (time duration) and the depth (capital need). For instance, a firm building a medical device must consider the need for regulatory approvals before the solution can be sold to customers. The capital needed for building such businesses is, therefore, higher.

All founders must deeply internalize the innovation adoption curve or product lifecycle curve and beware of the chasms on the way. It captures the growth in the number of active customers with time. The number of customers directly indicates revenue growth. One curve represents one product or service, i.e., one innovation. The different points on the curve identify various **milestones** in the product's development related to **customer adoption**. *Your firm's survival and growth depend on new customer adoption.* So, we must clearly and deeply understand who the beneficiary (user) is and who the customer (the one who would pay) is. *Developing the customer* is, therefore, the crucial first step in developing the business idea into a thriving firm. We shall refer to the product lifecycle curve throughout this book to understand the nature of a firm's development.

Gaining the early one-third customer base involves rightly characterizing the prospective customers. Even early adopters and early majority customers resist change, but for genuine reasons. For e.g., if the customer has recently invested in an alternative solution, they will want to wait for their renewal cycle opportunity (typically about four years) before they can rip and replace it with your improved solution. There is a switching cost (10) that you must take into account. If prospective customers resist accepting the innovation without a business reason, they may be in the late adopter or laggard category.

Innovators and early adopter customers are also more likely to switch out of your product to another emerging solution by their nature. Therefore, it is imperative to win customers beyond them quickly and not rely only on the initial customers.

FROM THE IDEA TO THE STARTUP JOURNEY

According to Steve Blank (11), a Silicon Valley startup guru and the originator of *customer development*, a startup is not a smaller version of a large company (12). Mature companies execute known and established business models. Startups have only a vision and conviction based on assumptions and unknowns. Not every new venture can be called a "startup." To be termed a startup, the firm must intend to grow and gain scale of operations quickly to grow its results non-linearly.

Steve Blank defines a startup as a *temporary organization in search of a scalable, repeatable, profitable business model.* The keyword here is "search"—it is about controlled, managed experiments prone to failures and learning from them. In this book, the **startup** is a clearly defined state in the lifecycle curve. It follows Steve Blank's definition and *extends the definition to add, "And needs external capital to execute its strategy for growth."* In this context, a startup can be an independent firm, or integral part of an established business that ventures into a new business opportunity (diversification) or initiating a business transformation such as *digital transformation.*

Even when a firm has a million *consumers*, it might have yet to achieve the business model fit and cannot sustain itself only on *customer* revenue. Such startups must bring the external capital to survive, add more customers and continue the search for a sustainable business model.

On the other hand, bootstrapped startups (13) build growth in the startup only using operating revenue, reinvesting from profits made. A lack of external capital might slow the development of the firm initially. However, it is a genuine approach to building long-term sustainable firms, as the firm learns to use capital efficiently as part of its DNA.

The journey from the idea (or proof of concept) to the startup state is searching for **problem-solution fit (PSF)**—it is the journey of customer discovery and PSF is the first major milestone to achieve.

THE JOURNEY THROUGH THE CHASMS AND LEARNING

In this book, we define the **thriving** state on the lifecycle curve as when *the firm has enough customer revenue to execute a reasonably predictable business plan, can sustain a rate of adding new customers, pay market-competitive compensation to all its employees, and can re-invest profits to sustain its innovation on the product roadmap.* The thriving state is the indicator of the *scalability* of the firm towards *maturity* and *market leadership*. At this stage, the firm has won with innovators, early adopters, and a part of the early majority—approximately a third or less of the maximum estimated customer base for the product. The *Lifetime Value (LTV)* of the customers to the firm is much greater than its *Customer Acquisition Cost (CAC)* and all other operating costs, and the firm achieves stable operating profits. During the work-in-progress, a bootstrapped firm is not to be confused with the thriving state, as the firm may not be *scalable* to address a larger marketspace or *sustainable* without key persons. At the thriving state, the firm has established scalability and sustainability also, and it is generating free cash flow from its revenues to sustain and grow according to its business plan.

There is an essential milestone after crossing the chasm known as Product-Market Fit or PMF. At PMF, the product is acceptable to the customers at its target price. PMF includes **Experience-Market Fit** (EMF) which is an indication of whether the ideal customer profile values the experience of the product delivery. Consider the difference between Rolex and Timex watches. Beyond PMF, the firm works toward the next milestone of a proven business model, or **Business Model Fit (BMF).** At this point, the firm is ready for scaling up, and some refer to the stage as **scaleup.**

We define scaleup stage as *initial design of an organization that has achieved a viable, repeatable, profitable and sustainable business model, ready to scale rapidly to grow in the market space.* The firm is now ready to scale up towards the thriving stage. The firm has overcome the *technology* and *market risks* and now must deal with the *execution risk* and *scalability risk*. The journey from idea to the thriving state is about **capital optimization**. During this part of the journey, the firm's goal is to use minimum capital to achieve customer adoption and milestones as defined on the product adoption curve. The focus must be on the **Quality** of the product, customer experience and revenue. Customer experience is beyond the essential utility and functionality of a product, and forms an essential part of achieving EMF. **Quality of Revenue** (QoR) is an objective analysis to build capability in the firm to generate consistent, predictable, and scalable growth in revenue streams and margins from the core product and customer experience.

This part of the journey is in the **box of innovation**. The growth of this firm during this period can be comparable to the part of our life of being in school. A lot of learning is the primary outcome, and your results depend primarily on your actions. You are only competing with the alternatives of early adopters to fulfil their needs and wants.

Technologists are naturally problem-solvers and implementers. That is their comfort zone. Their attention is likely to be more on building the product (the destination.) They often are oblivious to the fact that they are building a team and a firm (the vehicle.) Most first-time founders are underprepared to tackle this most challenging part of a product-based firm's lifecycle. You must develop a deeper understanding of why and how firms run out of cash or fail to raise new capital, especially in the earlier stages of your firm's development.

The journey through the box of innovation is the arduous journey of jumping over the chasms and one of rapid learning—somewhat like the school days, competing primarily with yourself. This book focuses on this part of the journey and climb. No one process guarantees success in reaching the PMF point (sometimes referred to as "0 to 1") and thriving state (referred to as "1 to 10x and beyond"). This book presents a rough sequence of milestones ("outcomes") and introduces approaches to get there.

JOURNEY FILLED WITH BATTLES

Once your firm is thriving, it naturally attracts competition. In the lifecycle curve, a product that scales up continues the journey from **thriving** toward **maturity** and **market leadership**. The journey transitions from the box of innovation to the **box of rapid growth**. The firm is ready to transform from an innovation mindset to establishing a scalable business system in transitioning from thriving towards maturity. The journey from thriving to a mature state is about building a scalable business system. Two essential battles characterize the journey past the thriving state—building the business system ("the battles inside") and winning against the direct competitors ("the battles outside.") The essential difference in the case of a scalable firm is its execution capability and preparedness for rapid scale up of capabilities with double-digit growth rates. A question to ask at this stage is: *What does it take us to deliver if our demand doubles, triples, quadruples?* During this part of the journey, the firm must focus on building **predictability** and **productivity** in that order. Now the firm is ready to prepare for an initial public offering (IPO) or to be acquired by a more prominent firm to accelerate monetization.

This transition from the thriving state to the maturity state presents a few deep chasms for the firm could fall through. In the thriving state, the firm starts to be well-known in the industry, and severe direct competition emerges as the firm is poised for profitable rapid growth. Continuously winning against direct competition and maturing the business systems for growth presents multiple chasms the firm must jump over.

The innovators that *create* thriving firms are not necessarily the ones that *scale* them up into large corporations. Evidence shows that only in minuscule instances did the founders scale up their firms toward market leadership. It is a proven strategy for many shrewd and larger corporations to bypass the radical and risky journey from an idea to a thriving state. Instead, they carefully watch or actively support developing startup firms rapidly moving toward a thriving state. These larger corporations acquire the innovating firms during their early phases when the market opportunity is enormous, and they expect to execute the business processes faster and more efficiently. These Corporations are the *fast-second* corporations (14). There are also numerous instances when such acquisitions fail, often due to cultural incompatibilities and premature scaling attempts before achieving PMF. Successful integration of an innovative team from a thriving startup into a larger firm, either through a friendly or hostile acquisition, is a huge change management challenge. This presents a deep chasm for the innovative product to become a thriving business unit in the larger corporation.

Hank Bernes (15) describes a chasm that emerges in the middle of the early majority adoption—before you get to the late majority. It is before the peak. We see issues for mature firms to get to market leadership in more than 50% of firms. The role of *marketing* and *innovation in the market* assumes a critical role in this journey.

BEWARE, MIND THE KNOWING-DOING GAP

Numerous books, articles, podcasts, startup support organizations, networks, and video recordings of great speakers are coming out every day, sharing entrepreneurship and business management knowledge and wisdom. Then why are some firms more successful than most? *Knowing what to do is not enough* (16). Jeffrey Pfeffer and Robert I. Sutton have published their findings on the "Knowing-Doing Gap," and their book is evergreen. Most leaders find it immensely challenging to translate performance knowledge into action on the ground, reflected in the business results. Imagine the last time you lost a game. Was it that you didn't know what to do? Or was it that you didn't do what you knew? Either may be the case, but more often, it is the latter.

We must internalize the *why* before the *how* is crucial to deal with this gap. Establishing an *early warning system (EWS)* among the team members and external advisors to observe and question us is a reasonable preventive measure against the knowing-doing gap.

Training your mind to listen empathetically and seek external help are proven ways to overcome the "knowing-doing" gap.

The most critical knowing-doing gap most founders fall into is about the *customers*—only customers make any firm a reality. Then, why are we not starting with the customers?

KEY TAKEAWAYS AND ACTION PLANNING

1. Innovations take time to get adopted. People participate differently in adopting any innovation, which is an emotional process. For any product to reach a good level of adoption, it must get about one-third of the estimated total possible customers.
2. Startup is a *temporary organization* in search of a scalable, repeatable, profitable, and sustainable business model. It requires external capital to execute the strategy rapidly to perform the search and reach the destination of a thriving state. Startup could also bootstrap to grow at a slower pace. The intent of a startup is to scale up and grow to capture most of the market opportunity, whereas a small enterprise does not necessarily have the serious intent to scale up.
3. Build your firm to deliver the product with quality and customer experience first, then seek predictably and improve it for productivity.
4. The idea grows to become a thriving firm in the box of *product innovation* and then grows further toward maturity in the box of rapid growth or *market innovation*.
5. Every new product idea starts with assumptions, including the price at which customers would buy the product. Only prospective customers can validate your assumptions.
6. Beware of the *chasms* or gaps that your firm can fall through. It would be best if you were well-prepared to cross each chasm.
7. Capital optimization characterizes the early part of the firm's journey.

8. In the *innovation box*, firm grows from *idea stage* to *startup*, then to *scaleup*, and to *thriving stage*, when it is ready to enter the *box of rapid growth*.
9. There needs to be more than just being aware of the *knowing-doing gap*. Know the "why" before the "how."

CALL TO ACTION

1. Establish a set of guiding principles for taking your idea towards building a firm. Based on what you learned, review and revise these principles once in six months.
2. Create a list of your fundamental assumptions about the idea, especially concerning its users and customers.
3. If you are already contemplating or executing a tech startup, identify its CRL. Create your roadmap to progress to the higher CRL levels, in terms of capital required and approximate time period. Think about ways to optimize the capital need and develop your strategy.
4. DeepTech ideas take substantial time before paying customers can be served (e.g., a medical device must go through several certifications before it can be sold commercially.) Therefore, the focus of such firms must be to develop and protect the intellectual property assets. Do you have an intellectual property strategy and capital allocated appropriately?

REFERENCES

1. https://www.sun-sentinel.com/sports/fl-xpm-2012-11-09-sfl-mike-tyson-explains-one-of-his-most-famous-quotes-20121109-story.html last accessed on 01-Jan-2022
2. https://www.sun-sentinel.com/sports/fl-xpm-2012-11-09-sfl-mike-tyson-explains-one-of-his-most-famous-quotes-20121109-story.html last accessed on 01-Jan-2022
3. Joseph A. Schumpeter, "Capitalism, Socialism and Democracy," 3rd Edition, 1950.
4. Bohlen, Joe M., Beal, George M. (May 1957). "The Diffusion Process." Special Report No. 18. 1: 56–77.
5. Frank M. Bass, "A New Product Growth for Model Consumer Durables," Management Science, Vol. 15. No. 5, January 1969, 215-227.
6. Geoffrey A. Moore, "Crossing the Chasm: Marketing and Selling Disruptive Products to Mainstream Customers," 3rd Edition, Harper Business, 2014, ISBN 978-0-062-35394-8.
7. Uday Phadke & Sam Dods, "Idea to Impact Research Programme, Working Paper 1/Part 2: Maturity Mapping, May 2022, downloaded from https://www.thetriplechasm.com/research last accessed 03-Sep-22.
8. Everett M. Rogers, "Diffusion of Innovations," 5th Edition, Simon and Schuster. 2003, ISBN 978-0-7432-5823-4, pp.1
9. Summary of Roger's Innovation Adoption Curve. Abstract: https://www.valuebasedmanagement.net/methods_rogers_innovation_adoption_curve.html last accessed 01-Sep-2022.
10. Nicholas Carr, "The Big Switch: Rewiring the World, From Edison to Google," 2009, W. W. Norton & Company, ISBN https://www.nicholascarr.com/?page_id=21
11. https://steveblank.com/about/ About Steve Blank accessed on 13-Jul-2022.
12. https://steveblank.com/2011/09/01/why-governments-

don%E2%80%99t-get-startups/ Steve Blank: Why Governments Don't Get Startups, posted Sept 1, 2011, accessed on 13-Jul-2022.
13. Will Kenton, "What is Bootstrapping? What it means and How It's Used in Investing," Investopedia, 07-Nov-2020, URL: https://www.investopedia.com/terms/b/bootstrapping.as p: Last accessed 01-Sep-2022.
14. Constantinos C. Markides, "Fast Second: How Smart Companies Bypass Radical Innovation to Enter and Dominate New Markets," Jossey-Bass, 2004, ISBN 978-078-7-971540.
15. Hank Barnes, https://blogs.gartner.com/hank-barnes/2021/09/28/the-democratization-of-technology-has-created-a-new-b2b-chasm/, last accessed 01-Sep-2022.
16. Jeffrey Pfeffer and Robert I. Sutton, "The Knowing-Doing Gap: How Smart Companies Turn Knowledge into Action," Harvard Business School Press, ISBN 1-57851-124-0, 2000.

3

WHERE IS YOUR CUSTOMER?

"The hard part about figuring out what customers want is figuring out that you need to figure it out."

— *Paul Graham, Founder and Partner of Y Combinator (1), in a short article, Schlep Blindness*

CHATTI CAN CHAT WITH ANYONE IN ANY LANGUAGE

Mary started her firm based on the inventions and ideas from her freshly minted AI research work for her Ph.D. Her thesis guide encouraged her dream of building a firm. Her university had access to small grants to promote entrepreneurship, and she could easily win a grant award. And Mary built the prototype using the grant money and started demonstrating the prototype in exhibitions and to visitors. People were amused and impressed by the idea of the *chatting robot* she built—C*hatti*.

Mary's guide felt confident, and he introduced her to a few industry veterans who could fund her firm. Mary met with them, and they all encouraged her. But asked her to get at least one buyer for Chatti. Mary was confused and felt helpless/angry. That is precisely what she needed the money for—to manufacture the robot robustly and to hire a salesperson to sell it. Now she is out of money to even sustain herself. How could she proceed? Mary went to her guide disappointed and wanted to report that all the contacts he gave were not helpful. But as she entered her guide's office, an older man was in the office. Mary had seen him on a few occasions before but never bothered to get introduced. Now, her guide introduced him to Mary as a brilliant technologist working somewhere. He can't provide any money, but possibly some advice. Mary wasn't keen to meet him, as she wasn't looking for any advice, especially from an oldie technologist who would perhaps tell his battle stories of assembly language coding. Mary needed just 250k USD to build the first production-quality robot ready to sell. But Mary decided to meet him with an open mind, once.

After the pleasantries, the man asked, *"Who will buy Chatti?"* Mary was a little irritated, *"Anyone who needs her help."* He persisted, *"Who is that person? What is the job he must get done with Chatti?"* Mary responded, *"Chatti is programmable. We can program her to many repetitive chat patterns in any language."* Chatti will do reasoning and will learn on the job. How cool is that! The question-answer continued, and Mary started to feel awkward and realized she lacked clarity about who needed the robot and why they would buy it. The man smiled and asked her what she did with her grant money. *"Built Chatti, the prototype. It was important to demonstrate the idea."* Mary responded. *"But you could have used that funding to discover a few customers, right?"* Mary was puzzled, *"Then what would I show them?"* The man said, *"Nothing. You would have understood the jobs they must do, the pains they suffer doing those jobs, and whether your robot is even relevant to them. You could have validated your assumptions and got some evidence to discover who your early customers can be."* Mary was skeptical but thoughtful. *"You wanted me to do that? I wanted to hire a salesperson to talk to customers after we are ready to produce and sell... But..."* The man nudged Mary to think. The dialog continued for a long time. At the end of the meeting, Mary was ready to apply for the following grant—this time to do *Customer development*. And after several months, a well-dressed Shuka receives guests in five-star hotels and fine-dining restaurants—Shuka is powered by Chatti 3.0.

THIS BOOK IS NOT FOR EDISON

CHOOSING THE IDEA TO WORK ON IS NON-TRIVIAL

Everything starts with a founder choosing to work on an idea. The big question is how to figure out if building a startup is a good idea. If it is an *obviously* good idea, it solves a well-known problem. Big companies and numerous people are already working on it (e.g., how to extend the life of batteries?) Your startup will essentially be on a race to finish with the strong players, and why would you win?

So, it would be best if you chose to work on an idea that may not apparently look like a good business idea—it is counter-intuitive or contrarian thinking. It must solve an important problem for a large population to build a scalable firm around the idea. It is excellent to start with a clearly visible problem and design a new technical solution enabled by new technology capability (e.g., blockchain or generative AI.) Many DigitalTech firms naturally start this way or can easily follow this approach. Paul Graham writes about this challenge in a short article, *schlep blindness* (2). If you have a personal connection with the problem you choose to work on (e.g., you experience it, people known to you experience it, etc.,), it helps a great deal.

When you are picking an idea from your Ph.D. research work, typically, the idea is likely to be high on scientific novelty. But there may be no immediate real-world problem it solves. Well-designed DeepTech startups emanate from progressive university research that begins with an unsolved problem with a wide application in the industry (or large *market size*.) It is wise to do the market size calculations upfront and choose the problem, not at the end of your Ph.D. program, for easier commercialization of the research outcome.

When your idea comes out of deep industry experience in the domain, it is likely easy for you to size the market opportunity. In that case, the time and capital to develop the scientific novelty and intellectual property assets are more challenging. It would be best if you created a detailed roadmap for your journey from idea to thriving state, which will maximize operating revenue and optimize capital. Doing a Ph.D. can be a strategy to develop the new technology proof of concept and eliminate the technology risk.

Good startup ideas are well-developed, multi-year plans that contemplate many possible paths according to how the world changes. Balaji Srinivasan calls this the *idea maze* (3) (4). Tech founders must invest the time to develop a deep understanding of the landscape of their idea—the history of the industry, other players, how technology development is changing the existing landscape, previous initiatives, and so on through *secondary research* and, when possible, *primary research* conversing with experts in the domain.

UNDERSTAND YOUR CUSTOMER BEFORE YOU HAVE ONE

Ideas are solutions to a perceived or experienced problem. We get excited and begin to build the solution too soon, create a demo, and tell the story, raise the money, and scale. This is the root cause of most startup failures. Every new business idea is essentially a bunch of assumptions, some of which are *killer assumptions*. You can't challenge or validate your assumptions in your lab or worktable. As Steve Blank says, *"Get out of the building!"* (5).

In the context of entrepreneurship, in all cases, it is crucial to establish a strong foundation for your idea before you start building the solution. It is to formulate the problem your idea is proposing to solve. Ideally, this must be completed before the founder leaves their current occupation. Successful founders are *optimistic realists*—triggered by intuition, but they validate with facts—data, observed behaviors, etc.

Common risks observed with technology-focused founders are:

- Assuming everyone suffers the problem and is looking for a solution immediately.
- A belief that customers must experience a new product before they can say how much they will pay for it.
- Trying to solve too many problems for too many types of customers.

THIS BOOK IS NOT FOR EDISON

The only *entity* who can answer all your questions and help you validate your assumptions is the **beneficiary user** and the **customer** (the one who pays you.) We shall refer to both together as "**customer**" unless there is a need to separate. There are only two effective ways to do this.

- Talk directly to your customers and partners and observe their behaviors.
- Design and run experiments to put people through experiences and observations.

Founders have many excuses for not meeting their customers—"*I don't have anything to show; we are not ready with our demo; I will talk to them when the minimum viable product is ready,*" and so on. The real reason is a fear of facing reality—moving from the world of abstraction to the world of real people. It is only postponing the problem to a later day when the cost of solving it is much higher. *Not establishing the problem* is a major defect in the startup process, and it is the cheapest to solve it earliest in the life cycle.

This activity is referred to as *Customer Discovery* and what follows is called *Customer Validation*, (6) and it leads to a clear product vision. The typical questions at this stage are:

- What specific problem does your solution ("the idea") solve?
- Who has this problem?
- When do they experience or suffer the problem?
- Who can confirm they suffer from this problem?
- What are they doing about this problem now?
- How much does the problem cost them now? (Time, money, etc.)
- If we solve this problem, what will impact the customer's business or life?
- What is the customer trying to get done or experience (what is the "job to be done?")
- Are they willing and able to pay for the solution?

- Who will pay?
- How much will they be willing to pay?

Your conversation with the customer should not be asking these questions directly but developing the insights through an open-ended dialog in the context of the customer. Customer discovery meetings must be in person, as much as possible—in the same room, via video call, or by phone: no email surveys, no group discussions.

You are not pitching anything at this stage. Instead, you must be ready to listen and learn. And it is essential that the founder does these discussions personally and not delegate. Your customer is always a human being, not a company. If your idea is to serve a business enterprise, identify who within the enterprise is the person who is likely to suffer the problem. We use the term *persona* to refer to the customer's role within their organization or decision-making group (e.g., Head of Manufacturing, Working woman.) We also must observe the *archetype* within the customer organization for the persona (e.g., end-user, decision-maker, economic buyer, influencer, recommender, etc.) We use the term "customer" for simplicity. The customer persona and archetype details must be captured as part of the customer meeting notes.

Look through your network and take help to reach out to as many customers as possible to get a conversation opportunity. Plan your meeting meticulously to use the time well, based on what you want to learn and what you want to uncover about the problem.

One of the essential concepts to internalize before customer discovery interviews is about customers' *jobs to be done* (JTBD.) Origins of the JTBD concept point to a business professor Theodore Levitt, who said, *"People don't want a quarter-inch drill; they want a quarter-inch hole."* This quote captures the quintessential JTBD: focus on the outcome the customer is seeking, not your solution or technology. People buy products to get something done for themselves—accomplish tasks (and outcomes,) achieve their goals or objectives, resolve and avoid problems, entertain themselves, express themselves, etc.

Once you discover the JTBD associated with your innovation, you can find the *pains* associated with them—the markers of the problem your solution targets to solve. JTBD offers a unique lens for observing the customers you serve. JTBD helps you focus on what people try to achieve in each situation. Customers buy a product or service to get a job done. It has nothing to do with your solution. JTBD is solution-agnostic and stable over time. It is an indicator of the value of the innovation for them—you can define metrics more easily to measure success. Tony Ulwick introduced the JTBD framework (7) (8) (9) in 1991, and Prof. Clayton Christensen also popularized it through his work (10).

Ask about the problem you feel they have. Ask open-ended questions about the past and present, not the future. Only those answers are likely to be facts. This conversation may open other problems they consider more critical associated with the problem you are exploring. Or you may discover other issues related to the problem that calls for your solution re-targeted ("pivot") to another problem or context. Listen to their stories and experience. People may not be aware of the existence of the problem sometimes. Expose the problem in such cases by building awareness of the problem.

One of the common mistakes founders make is to meet too few potential beneficiaries of the solution. Meeting as many potential beneficiaries as possible would only do more good. How are they solving the problem today? Understand if they have put aside money to solve the problem or failed in their previous attempts. These are good indicators of the importance of the problem for the customer. What is the economic impact of the problem today— quality, reputation, time, effort, money, etc.? Is there a specific time for them to buy the solution? (e.g., budget cycle, school year.)

It is not helpful to ask questions about the future; sometimes, it can be misleading. Never ask something like, "*Will you buy if there is a solution to this problem today?*" Whatever your customer answers that question, it remains a hypothesis. When you build the solution based on the answer, the customer's situation could be different, or the relative priority for the solution may be low. Therefore, better questions to ask would be to establish the relative business impact of the problem on the customer personally and the business (e.g., would the customer's job be in danger without the solution?)

You must meet thirty to fifty people associated with the problem who can be your potential customers. Draw your insights from each meeting and make plans for the pivots. You should analyze about twenty customer interviews to observe problem space patterns. Synthesize your meeting notes to start forming the benefits you must offer from the customer's perspective. Now you can validate or invalidate some of your key assumptions. When you are inconclusive, do more customer interviews.

Giff Constable's "Talking to Humans" is an excellent reference for developing your competence in customer interviews. (11) Customer interviewing is a dialog to validate your assumptions about the customer's jobs, pains, and unmet needs. Marc McNeill (12), Sean Murphy (13), and Giff Constable (14) give several guidelines for preparing and conducting yourself during customer interactions.

EXPERIMENTS LEAD TO STRONGER EVIDENCE

Besides conversing with customers, designing experiments can yield more substantial evidence to validate hypotheses. However, designing experiments is harder and calls for creativity. The experiment is a temporary process to test the hypothesis. It is not the product or its scaled-down version. One way to experiment is to put people through a new experience and observe their reactions. The essential property of a good experiment is to help make better decisions.

The product's price is the most reliable indicator of the value of your solution. Starting the discussion about price before the product is developed helps you *design and build your solution around a price*. When all the information is available, and the decision-making is strictly rational, the price and value would converge. In reality, the difference between the price and value is based on perceptions and emotions, supported by rationale, most often communicated post the buying decision!

ASSESS THE ECONOMIC OPPORTUNITY, VALIDATING ASSUMPTIONS

At this stage, you only have an idea and many assumptions, including who needs the solution. What you are doing is validating or invalidating your assumptions. To do this, you don't need to build or show the solution. Instead, it would help if you validated your assumptions systematically as hypotheses. The essential difference between an assumption and a hypothesis is that the latter is logical and explicit. Here is a suggested structure to frame a logical hypothesis.

We believe that <your assumption.>
To verify that, we will <do something>.
And measure <something>.
We are right if <a condition is satisfied.>

Consider your idea to build a drill jig that can accurately guide drills. As a result, it significantly improves the production yield while drilling holes in steel plates. An example of a corresponding hypothesis statement to validate is: We believe *there is a high rejection rate in less sophisticated factories when drilling holes.* To verify that, we will *collect the rejection data from factories where drilling is done using low-end drilling machines.* And measure *the production yield %.* We are correct if *the yield is less than 75%.*

While defining your hypothesis, identify whether it is a "killer hypothesis"—meaning, if it is invalidated, your solution (idea) may not be relevant or valuable to the customer.

Following the customer interviews, record the learning corresponding to the hypothesis as follows:

We observed <what did we observe?>
From that, we learned that <what did we learn?>
Therefore, we will <take this action, pivot, etc.>

As we test our hypothesis with customer responses, validated hypotheses become facts that form the foundation for our solution design. Now test and assess whether the resulting business opportunity is repeatable and scalable. That is *Customer Validation*. If the value of the idea is not established in customer validation, pivot the solution, and return to customer discovery. We proceed forward and continue only if the customer validation succeeds.

The value of new ideas cannot be proven only using analytical methods. Market analysis approach will bubble up only incremental ideas on established products as their markets are well understood. Completely new ideas, e.g., Facebook when it was introduced, cannot be proven using analytical means.

WHERE IS MY FIRST LOVE?

As you cross thirty to forty customer interviews and systematically analyze the findings, your mind will start seeing the patterns. You can begin to synthesize your learning. You might have concluded on many hypotheses. If things encourage you to pursue your idea, keep continuing the search to learn more. You have learned a lot, and it is time to make some decisions. If the customers mostly discourage you in the context of the idea, it is time to think deeper. If the customers convinced you that your idea was irrelevant in the market and that you are no longer passionate about it, you saved your life at a meager cost! Look for the next new idea. Long live the new idea!

ARE YOU RUNNING FAST, IN THE WRONG DIRECTION

You must establish your market opportunity before you develop your technology and product, grow your team, establish a brand, and design your marketing materials, including your website, and so on. As you discover your customers and their JTBDs, you can start clustering them into *customer segments* or *market space domains* based on their type, needs, financial profile, etc. Market opportunities can vastly differ in their *attractiveness* to the firm—based on the value creation potential and your challenge to capture the value. You must assess your firm's capabilities to deliver in the context of the market space, and it need not stay static forever. Choose a *primary* market space domain after a careful analysis. The analysis should also illuminate other segments you could pursue concurrently without significant additional resources.

Market Opportunity Navigator (15) (MON) guides you through this 3-step process with a visual, easy-to-apply framework. MON is most applicable to discover the best commercialization strategy for technology inventions (DeepTech, and technology transfer of research outcomes.) Three dedicated worksheets (free downloadable) help you to ask the right questions and discover your best choices. The creators of MON have created a free web application **app.wheretoplay.com**, to help using this process.

Remember, great ideas are often *contrarian*. Are you still convinced about the idea's value but unable to connect it to the jobs to be done and the customers' pains? Then define the new set of hypotheses based on what you have learned. Is the problem you are trying to solve not acknowledged? Then perhaps you are too disruptive and unable to internalize the people issues involved in adopting your idea. Continue your search and stay in the customer discovery and validation loop. Your firm's pathway to profitability lies in fully understanding your customer and delivering an experience the customer wants more.

Innovative founders manage to create demand. They create products that customers didn't even know they wanted or had ever imagined. However, such solutions connected well with a *latent* JTBD. When the first airplane took off, there was no inherent demand for flying, because it was practically impossible. The JTBD is moving from one place to another, as quickly as possible at an affordable cost. Customer development is not asking Customers to specify what we should build—that is *contract engineering*. Customer discovery is about connecting our solution with the customer's needs/wants (establishing the demand). Customer development is about building the business model and a firm to deliver it.

If you are the lucky one successful in establishing the demand, go ahead. Let's discuss the solution now!

KEY TAKEAWAYS AND ACTION PLANNING

1. Choosing the right idea to work on is non-trivial.
2. Understand your customer before you have one. A lot can be done with your prospective customers before building your product.
3. Customers do not buy a product or service. They buy solutions to their problems (needs) or fulfilling their desires (wants.) Internalize the concept of JTBD.
4. Buying is an emotional decision, not just a rational decision. Often the decision is justified with a rationale.
5. *Price* is an essential hypothesis to validate with prospective customers.
6. Experiments provide more robust evidence for proving or disproving your hypothesis.
7. You must discover innovator and early adopter customers to start traction. Only a few people who suffer from the problem will become early customers, and be willing to co-develop the new solution, tolerating the teething troubles.

CALL TO ACTION

Before building your solution, you must validate the following assumptions.

1. Can you find *customers* trying to solve the problem you are proposing to solve for them right now? (Early adopters of your solution)
2. Can you understand their problem and speak their language when communicating your solution?
3. Are they open to taking your help solving it?
4. Are they willing and able to pay for the solution?
5. Do you have evidence that they have already sought a solution by investing their time and money?
6. Will the proposed price the prospective customer will pay yield

positive gross profit, ideally above 50%? Remember, "Low price" is not a differentiator, but a losing business strategy for startup; but "low cost" is a result of innovation. Founders must resist the tendency to price their product low to win early customers but offer a visible discount to co-developers and early adopters, and account it as cost of customer acquisition.

If you cannot get affirmative, positive answers to these questions, it is not wise to progress further to build the product. And to get answers to the above questions, you don't need to build the product.

REFERENCES

1. Found as a quote in a book. Original source could not be found.
2. Paul Graham, "Schlep Blindness," URL: http://www.paulgraham.com/schlep.html: Last accessed 01-Oct-2022.
3. Chris Dixon, "The Idea Maze," 04-Aug-2013, URL: https://cdixon.org/2013/08/04/the-idea-maze: Last Accessed 01-Sep-2022. Please read this blog post and the detailed paper by Balaji Srinivasan if you are unfamiliar with the concept of the idea maze.
4. Balaji Srinivasan, "Market Research, Wireframing, and Design," URL: https://spark-public.s3.amazonaws.com/startup/lecture_slides/lecture5-market-wireframing-design.pdf: Last accessed 01-Sep=2022.
5. Steve Blank and Bob Dorf, "The Startup Owner's Manual: The Step-By-Step Guide for Building a Great Company," 1st Edition, Wiley, Amazon Kindle Edition, 2020, ISBN 978-0-9849993-7-8.
6. Steve Blank and Bob Dorf, "The Startup Owner's Manual: The Step-By-Step Guide for Building a Great Company," 1st Edition, Wiley, Amazon Kindle Edition, 2020, ISBN 978-0-9849993-7-8.
7. Tony Ulwick article: https://jobs-to-be-done.com/jobs-to-be-done-a-framework-for-customer-needs-c883cbf61c90, last accessed 01-Sep-22.
8. Anthony W. Ulwick, "Jobs to be done: Theory to Practice," Idea Bite Press, 2016, ISBN 0-9905767-5-4.
9. Jim Kalbach, "The Jobs to be Done Playbook: Align Your Markets, Organization, and Strategy around Customer Needs," 1st edition, Two Waves Books; 2020, Amazon Kindle Edition, 978-1-933820-68-2.
10. Clayton Christensen "The Theory of Jobs to be done,"

URL: https://hbswk.hbs.edu/item/clay-christensen-the-theory-of-jobs-to-be-done: last accessed 01-Sep-2022.
11. Giff Constable, "Talking to Humans: Success starts with understanding your customers," 1st edition, Amazon Kindle Edition, 2014, ISBN 978-0-9908009-1. Please read this book for details and best practices for effective customer discovery interviews.
12. Marc McNeill, "Twelve Tips for Customer Development Interviews," http://www.dancingmango.com/blog/2012/12/14/twelv-tips-for-customer-development-interviews/, last accessed 10-Sep-2022.
13. Sean Murphy, "40 Tips for B2B Customer Development Interviews," https://www.skmurphy.com/blog/2020/01/30/40-tips-for-b2b-customer-development-interviews/, last accessed 10-Sep-2022.
14. Giff Constable, "12 Tips for Early Customer Development Interviews," http://giffconstable.com/2012/12/12-tips-for-early-customer-development-interviews-revision-3/ last accessed 10-Sep-2022.
15. The Market Opportunity Navigator, https://wheretoplay.co, Last accessed 01-Oct-2022. The book reference is Marc Gruber, Sharow Tal, "Where to Play: 3 Steps for Discovering Your Most Valuable Market Opportunities," Pearson India, 2019, ISBN 978-93-534-3001-6.

SUNDARA NAGARAJAN

4

LEAD WITH YOUR PURPOSE AND VISION

"Only the paranoid survive."

– *Andrew Grove, CEO, Intel Corporation.*

NAREN TURNED AROUND HIS FIRM

Naren had left a fantastic career with his employer to start this firm. He is investing his money to build the initial prototype he is passionate about. And a few good friends put their money into encouraging and supporting Naren's idea. But no customer seems to care. Naren's firm had succeeded in pilots with a few customers, but each one wanted different features for them to use the product. There was no venture capital interest. As Naren felt helpless and disappointed, he discovered the customer discovery and development process. That was the turning point. He and his team engaged with the customers passionately, this time to listen and understand the customer's problem space and the *jobs to be done*, and not to pitch the product. Based on what they learned, they made strategic choices of the niche they wanted to position their solution. They could communicate their value proposition effectively, using *the customer's words*. In a few months, Naren's firm won three paying customers, and the customers referred Naren's firm to their professional friends. Naren has rejuvenated his ailing infant firm. He realized that he must deeply understand the customer's problems and desires before building the solution. And ultimately, it is the product that delivers value and fulfils the Customer's needs and wants.

DEVELOP YOUR IDEA INTO CUSTOMER VALUE

When you have completed the customer discovery, you are ready to analyze what you found and design your *value proposition* for the customers and your firm's *business model*. Alexander Osterwalder and Yves Pigneur's contributions on value proposition design (1) and business model (2) generation are relevant now. They conceived the *Value Proposition Canvas* and *Business Model Canvas* as thinking frameworks to *capture* and *validate* your assumptions. These frameworks help visualize and design your value proposition and business model.

All ideas at the earliest stage of development are best guesses or assumptions yet to be validated among customers and the marketplace. We can compute or imagine the consequences of these guesses when they are proven true and what results (benefits) they could deliver to people. However, we must compare these results with observations and measurements from experiments and experience. If the measurements disagreed with our imagination, we were probably wrong with our idea. Learning this earlier is better than later after we have spent a lot of time and capital. Therefore, our approach is *capital optimization* during the early growth phases.

Which assumptions should we validate first? Following is a recommended order of validating assumptions, following the business model canvas elements.

1. Start with Ideal Customer Profile (ICP) for the Value Proposition, define Customer Segments or Market Space domains fit with the value proposition.(Problem-Solution Fit)
2. Customer Relationships & Channels (How do we reach our ideal customers?)
3. Key Activities & Resources (How do we prepare our solution? Planning talent and financial capital and the operating model)
4. Key Partners (How do we deliver our solution? Leveraging the ecosystem)
5. Revenue Streams & Cost Structures (What is the financial perspective? Financial model and rolling forward forecast.)

To validate assumptions concerning the Customer Segments and Value Proposition, we can use the Value Proposition canvas framework with the following elements.

1. Customer Jobs to be done
2. Pains (3) & Pain relievers
3. Gains & Gain Creators
4. Product Capabilities

We shall see more details of value proposition design and business modeling in Chapter 6.

Before we started the customer discovery, we would fill up the Value Proposition Canvas and the Business Model Canvas with our guesses and assumptions articulated as *hypotheses*. A hypothesis is an assumption made explicitly, along with how to validate or invalidate it.

For example, *we believe there is a high rejection rate* while drilling holes of tolerance $\pm$ 0.001 units. *To verify that, we will* collect the rejection data from factories. *And measure* the yield %. *We are right if* the yield is < 80%. Please note the quantitative way of articulating the hypothesis to validate it. A suggested template for articulating a

hypothesis is as follows (4).
We believe that…To verify that we will…And measure…We are right if …

If your idea's validity and relevance are anchored on a hypothesis, it should be identified as a *killer hypothesis*. If this riskiest assumption is invalidated through experiments or experience, the idea may not be worth pursuing in its current form. Therefore, such a hypothesis must be conclusively validated before making investments to develop the prototype. Capture the learning from the hypothesis validations through customer interviews and experimentation. Such learnings can help refine the hypothesis regarding the problem space. An adequate hypothesis should be about the problem space, its economic impact, the decision-making process for adopting the solution, and so on.

The emergence of solutions such as *Facebook, Twitter,* and other components of the Social-Mobile-Analytics-Cloud (SMAC) paradigm can be discovered in hindsight as a series of experiments with the people, rapid learning from early adoptions, and a series of innovations. The *Lean Startup* (5) principles emerged during this era of software innovations. The essence of the lean startup approach is *inexpensive product iterations to reduce wastage.* Lean startup and agile practices require adaptation or may not be applicable in developing products in DeepTech, complex product, or process development (e.g., a new semiconductor manufacturing process.)

KNOW YOUR NEXT MILESTONE

We start the journey with customer discovery and exploring the problem space using first principles. Getting affirmative, positive answers to the questions in the "Call to Actions" section of the previous chapter is a good indicator to start the journey to the next milestone. You have ascertained the problem and found a few early adopter customers who are willing to engage in developing the solution. When you have more clarity on the Problem-Solution Fit (PSF) it is time to build the initial prototype of your solution. In a "software-only" solution, this indicates the time to start building the *minimum viable product* (MVP). In a DeepTech scenario, we ask, *"Can we build and deploy the product that can solve the problem?"* and demonstrate the solution in the lab first. Following that, we are ready to answer the question, *"Can we solve the problem by delivering a product that uses this technology?"* Customer discovery must precede expensive prototype development, field trials, etc.

You must now move towards the next milestone, the "Product-Market Fit (PMF)." The term PMF came from the venture capital community (6) (7) and many others have interpreted and refined the definition. For our purpose, let us adopt Justin Wilcox's definition: *"PMF is satisfying a market that satisfies you."*

I like this definition because it also embeds the pricing and Founder-Market Fit (FMF) aspects. Following this definition, PMF is about finding the synergy between meeting the customer's and the founder's goals. PMF is an intuitively appealing concept in the lifecycle of a new product. But PMF is not a binary concept or a definitive milestone. When PMF happens, you feel it in many ways, and the most evident indicator is when your customers become your Salesforce. A reliable indicator of PMF is the *increasing trend of incoming customer leads converted* or demand due to customer referrals and campaigns.

Before we move on, a few myths must be busted. Being the *first mover* may not be an advantage. The likelihood of failure reduces by about five times if you are a *quick follower* or *improver*. Another myth is that highly creative (non-conformist) entrepreneurs like Steve Jobs do not do customer development or PMF. It is not true (8). Suppose your solution has high creativity-led content like Apple products or scientific inventions like a new medical device. In that case, you must build a prototype to help the customers experience the product. However, nothing close to the final product should be built in the first iteration. Creating a short movie of 3-5 minutes depicting the new experience with your solution is an economic way to validate and receive early customer/stakeholder feedback for your idea.

Business Model Canvas is a powerful companion framework to

develop the business strategy. Roger L. Martin (14) conceptualizes strategy as *a thinking process that results in either the reaffirmation of the choices you have already made, or the making of new set of choices that are different than the choices that inform and guide what you are doing today.* As you populate your business model canvas, capture your assumptions and choices, which forms your business strategy.

The crucial aspect to remember is *intuition* versus *data or evidence* in decision-making. When deeply experienced in a domain, your intuition is likely to be more right as intuition develops on data accumulated over time. Even then, the intuition must be validated before investing a lot of money in building the product. In other words, do *customer development* to validate your hypotheses by gathering evidence from the ICP users; or your startup may turn out to be an expensive failed experiment.

KNOW YOUR ALTITUDE, WATCH OUT FOR CHASMS

We now know the existence of the chasms (or voids) during the journey from the idea to establishing a successful firm. Uday Phadke and Shailendra Vyakarnam led a detailed study with thousands of startups and have developed the Triple Chasm Model (TCM) (9). The Commercialization Readiness Levels (CRL) (10) described as part of the Triple Chasm Model (TCM) offers a model that fits well for DeepTech and more complex product/process development efforts of firms.

As you are doing the customer discovery interviews, be alert to how the customer (customer's organization in the case of B2B) engages with you. We saw Roger's innovation adoption distribution earlier. Specifically, look for the innovators and earlier early adopters. Based on what you experienced, you can categorize your customers as follows.

- **Proto Customer**: early adopter customer willing to co-develop the product with you. They are willing to be alpha or beta customers and may contribute towards product development costs. *Lead users* also are categorized as proto-customers—these are innovators who discover an important problem in their life and create a solution to build for improving their life. Some lead users choose to become founders to build their idea into a product.

- **Charter-Customer**: early adopter customer who is not willing to co-develop the product but is ready to be an adopter once the product is in production or willing to do unpaid PoC with references from earlier customers. They contribute to refining the proposition and business model development.
- **Normal Customers**: Requires some education to adopt the solution. They engage with full commercial terms and SLAs and will pay based on an established business model.
- **NaC**: Not-a-Customer—either is not any of the above, has strong resistance to the innovation adoption, or has no budget for at least 24 months. 30-40% or even more of your customer interviews may indicate NaC. It is an opportunity to discover alternative solutions to the problem you may be unaware of.

This terminology is adopted from the TCM (11), which we shall use in this book when referring to customers. The TCM research indicates that the first two customer categories account for only 10% of total customer numbers. The proto customers will acknowledge the problem and are ready to spend effort and money with you to solve the problem. You will find only 2-3 proto customers when you meet over fifty. Founders must contribute directly to validating their ideas by validating their assumptions and discovering the customers.

CRL *	Commercialisation Readiness Level Definition	Lifecycle Curve
0	You are doing research on fundamental science and technology building blocks that could have a future application.	
1	You have started the process of thinking about how your science and technology could lead to a future product or service.	
2	You have identified a specific opportunity space where you could create a new product or service.	Customer development
3	You have created a product or service *concept* for the identified opportunity space (validated "idea".)	Startup Stage
	CHASM I	Proto development
4	You have successfully tested your completed prototype or demonstrator with *proto-customers*.	PSF
5	You have turned the prototype into a functioning product or service which reflects the feedback from proto-customers and it is generating initial revenues with *charter customers*.	
6	You have a product or service ready for deployment with *charter customers* with clarity on functionality, packaging and pricing, and you are exploring different *business models* and *channels to market*.	
	CHASM II	
7	You have demonstrated acceptance of your product or service with *charter customers* and you have developed a *sustainable business model* with ideas for potential channels to the market.	MDP development PMF/EMF
8	You have figured out how you are going to move from *charter customers* to *mainstream customers*, and you have defined your *channels to market* to support your *sustainable business model*.	
9	You are ready for full-scale deployment with *mainstream customers* with the functionality, packaging, pricing, *business model*, and *channels to market* pinned down.	Scaleup Stage
	CHASM III	
10	You are in full scale deployment with *mainstream customers* based on a *sustainable business model* and clear *distribution strategy*.	Mainstream adoption BMF/QofR

* CRL adapted from NASA Technology Readiness Level (TRL) approach
CRL is adapted in this book with permission from Triple Chasm Company, UK.

The NASA Technology Readiness Level (TRL) is well-known among technology researchers as a framework for assessing the maturity level of technology (12). However, TRL is limited in scope as it mainly concerns the maturity of the technology from idea to production and deployment. The CRL described as part of the TCM has extended the scope to cover the journey of an idea to the thriving stage of a firm. This book recommends the CRL model for assessing the progression of technology-based ventures. Reaching CRL7 is the earliest indication of PMF, and your firm is now ready for scaling up. TCM identifies *three distinct chasms* in the progression of the idea toward a thriving business.

The concept of MVP and PMF are intuitively appealing, and it fits well for software/internet solutions. These concepts need adaptation for DeepTech or research commercialization and products involving hardware, quality standard certifications, and so on (for example, medical devices.) For instance, the MVP for a medical device is a lab prototype with minimal use and cannot be given widely to customers for trials. The *minimum saleable product (MSP)* must have the manufacturing processes, certifications, and regulatory approvals. MSP is the prototype that can be deployed to proto-customers. This is the version of the product that is suitable for limited use by target users. The *minimum deployable product (MDP)* mapped to CRL6, is often the point of *launching* the product. It requires arrangements for consumables, servicing, etc. In the case of e-commerce services, MDP is the production quality implementation of a minimal product that can handle transactions and support consumers. MDP is ready for deployment to charter-customers. The firm can receive revenue from sales at this point.

The capital optimization approach is to link capital spend to validating hypotheses and creating deliverables (CRL levels,) rather than specific schedule. For e.g., launch the MDP (CRL6) within 100K USD, rather than by 01-Sep-2023. Timeline can be secondary target in startups, and capital primary.

GO AFTER THE LOW-HANGING FRUITS

Once you have completed a substantial number of customer discovery and validation interviews and experiments, you can start grouping customers into *customer segments* (grouping customers in a similar context.) You are also ready to articulate the first version of your *ideal customer prospect* or *ideal customer profile (ICP.)* Defining and refining ICP helps develop the *marketing (outreach, lead generation)* and *sales (order booking) process* in the future as the product achieves PMF. Until PMF is achieved, what we do to sign up customers is *Business Development*—the less structured process of *customer-driven innovation*, which the founder best executes.

After you have performed customer discovery and validation, you must now choose the customer segment to focus initially on. As a startup, you have limited resources and must apply that to the highest return opportunity. Typical considerations to make that choice are:

- Market size, determined by the number of unique customers.
- Your access (ease of reaching the decision-makers.)
- Customer's willingness and ability to pay.
- Relative business priority to solve the problem in the customer's context.

So far, you have stayed in the problem domain and established the existence of the problem your idea can solve. You know who suffers from that problem, and there may be an opportunity to make money solving that problem. We are ready to present our idea and its *value proposition* to the customer.

NOW YOU ARE COMPETING WITH YOURSELF

The climb from idea to thriving is like being in school—you are competing primarily with yourself. While competitive analysis is essential to discover your niche, competition is unlikely to kill you in this phase. Watch the competitive landscape and beyond to learn and establish your benchmarks. But the reasons for the firm to die in this phase of the journey are often internal (e.g., bad cash management, differences among founders, etc.) Reaching the thriving state is like graduating from school and entering a profession. It will be competitive from now on, and competition can kill the firm. *Start worrying about your competition only when your customers mention them to you. Until then, benchmark your perceived competition.* The following framework helps analyze the competitive landscape for an early-stage venture.

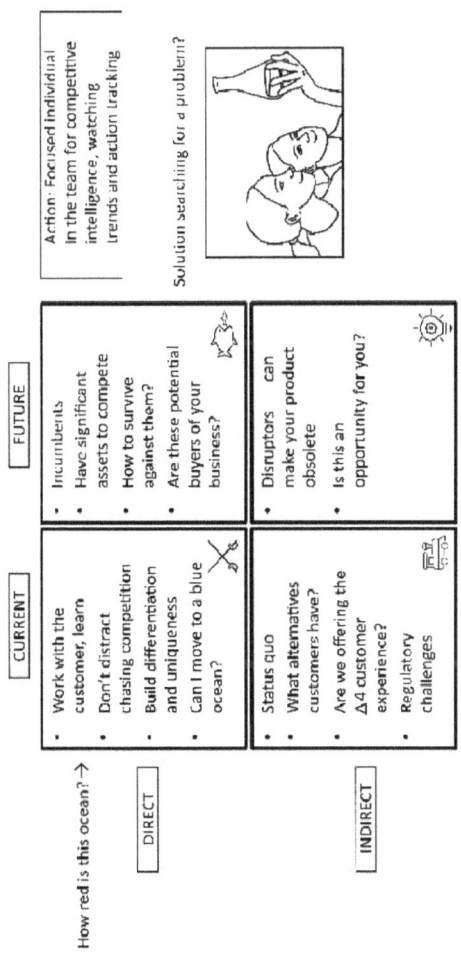

First, you categorize your competition as *current-direct* and *current-indirect* competitors. While current-direct competition is easier to understand, the current-indirect competition is tricky and more problematic. Of course, it includes the *status quo*. For DeepTech and

DigitalTech startups, the current indirect competition is significant to analyze. Kunal Shah articulates this situation through his *delta-4 theory* (13). The essence of the delta-4 theory is about heuristically *quantifying the resistance the new idea must overcome before it can be adopted in a specific context of alternatives.* The delta-4 theory applies mainly when a new idea is being targeted to new geo territories where the cost structures are dramatically different and existing alternatives are efficient.

Remember, what competes to win the customer's heart is the product, not the firm. Pixel 7 competes with iPhone 14. That is why startups have a fair opportunity to disrupt a large company in their marketspace. Have you heard of Blackberry smartphone?

ON INTERACTING WITH EARLY ADOPTERS

Use *customer discovery* when you are starting with technology and product. Starting with your inventions such as those from academic or industrial research labs, or your creative mind falls in this category. Use *design thinking* when you have established the problem, understand the customer well, and have a prototype ready. Delivering the best possible experience to the early adopters is the key to success in moving towards PMF. Design thinking helps that process.

The questions to focus on at this stage are:

- What are the customer segments (market opportunities) existing for us?
- What are the most attractive customer segments for us?
- Which customer segments should we focus on?
- How do we decide which opportunity to pursue first?

List your opportunities with a few attributes, such as the size of the opportunity space, how easy it is for you to contact them and market your solution, ease of getting paid, and so on. You can use a simple scoring scale such as 1 = Low, 2 = Medium, and 3 = High.

For instance, customers who have the pain your solution addresses and are rich will receive a "high" score. Prepare a table of customer segments and multiply your scores for each segment. A higher score indicates the appropriateness to pursue it as the initial Go-to-market opportunity space (target market space.) If any attribute is zero (e.g., no access to Government customers), score it as zero, and the opportunity is not for you.

Remember, this is a dynamic table, and the situation could change as time progresses. For instance, you may add a team member who understands and has relationships in the Government space, improving the score from zero to 2.

Founders wake up to the fact that their plan doesn't seem to survive the first customer contact. Sticking to a well-laid-out plan is nearly impossible. Creating an agile mindset and culture to respond to enhance the customer experience rapidly is essential. Usually, this phase of solving problems in the product based on customer feedback is relatively easy for startup teams compared to the earlier phases of customer development. However, many founders get distracted during this phase from serving customers to other initiatives such as public relations, competing for awards, etc., and lose out the early customer advocacy. The firm must focus on building quality and unique differentiation at this stage. When the firm gets to this stage of early customer engagement with the product, it is time to devote effort to convert the founder's foresight into its forecasts. The firm must build its predictability, building on the product quality it has achieved.

DESIGN EXPERIENCE, NOT PRODUCT

Creating an extraordinary product is about creating experience around the utility of the product. Can you develop insights about what your customer wants, before they do, and successfully design an experience most people couldn't imagine? To design disruptive experiences, founders must think beyond PMF. The JTBD method helps designers discover the customer's needs and wants from first principles. Designing **Experience-Market Fit (EMF)** is about removing friction in every step of consuming the *solution* the product and underlying technologies deliver. It is an *integrative design approach delivered with a highly empowered customer-facing team*. Understanding the customer profile deeply and pricing the experience appropriately is an essential part of achieving EMF. A well-designed EMF leads to products early adopters brag about and influence other people to adopt the experiences. In other words, true PMF in which your customers would feel disappointed and sad if your firm doesn't survive. Brian Hallign's paper (15) is a good place to start understanding the essential concepts behind designing superlative experience.

YOUR PURPOSE AND PASSION ARE YOUR FUEL

This phase of the startup is the hardest for most founders. Only a deep purpose toward the cause and your passion can keep you energized to overcome these chasms. You must be willing to continuously pivot, redesign and rehearse the communication until you start sensing the resonance from the customers and the indications of PMF and EMF.

The purpose of any startup is to serve its customers in the best possible way. Love your customer; and be empathetic. If you are a DigitalTech startup, you must find the right product for your customer, not the other way around. If you are a DeepTech startup, find the right customer for your product. And your purpose must be in this context.

When your journey reaches EMF, the next milestone is Business Model Fit (BMF.) Most technologist founders are energized by the innovations they do and the product they build. But, often, their engagement with the financial aspects of the firm may be relatively low. If you are oblivious to finance, it is time to wake up and learn to manage finance.

KEY TAKEAWAYS AND ACTION PLANNING

1. Designing the value proposition with the customer must precede product development.
2. Watch for the innovation adoption behavior of your prospective customers as you engage with them to validate your hypotheses—sign up proto and charter customers before you can expect normal customers to accept the new product.
3. Commercialization Readiness Level (CRL) helps you locate your firm's position in the journey. The firm progresses through different milestones and CRLs.
4. Your firm must discover Problem-Solution Fit (PSF), Product-Market Fit (PMF,) and Founder-Market Fit (FMF) in that order when it is ready to scale its capabilities to grow results.
5. This journey indicates crossing Chasms I and II. Chasm II is the hardest chasm to cross among all the chasms (transition from CRL6 to CRL7.)
6. Analyze the competitive choices for your Customers. Watch competitive choices to learn from initially. Build customer-centric thinking (my product vs. customer's JTBD.)
7. Discover the opportunity to deliver an experience around the basic utility the product delivers. Achieving Experience-Market Fit (EMF) is an optimum fit between the customer's emotional wants and your product's functional utility delivered by a highly empowered customer-facing team.

CALL TO ACTION

1. Establish progress indicators to help the firm accurately determine its position on the CRL scale. What is your position on CRL?
2. Design a way to find proto and charter customers in a sustainable and repeatable way appropriate to your product

and customers.

3. Discuss pricing as early as possible during the customer discovery interviews as you approach PSF. It will help you develop the product around pricing and optimize the features around the benefits customers' value.
4. Will you get a non-binding Letter of Intent (LoI) or establish a Memorandum of Understanding (MoU) with the prospective customer? Will you get pre-orders or advance payment for the product sale? These are reasonable ways to test whether your customers are willing to pay for your solution.
5. Establish measures of product quality and metrics that indicate customer engagement.
6. Create a definition of PMF and EMF for your firm. What success would look like?
7. Can you start estimating the Customer Life Time Value (LTV), Customer churn, Customer Acquisition Cost (CAC), etc.?

REFERENCES

1. Alexander Osterwalder and Yves Pigneur, "Value Proposition Design: How to Create Products and Services Customers Want," Wiley, 2014, ISBN 978-1-118-96805-5.
2. Alexander Osterwalder and Yves Pigneur, "Business Model Generation: A Handbook for Visionaries, Game Changers, and Challengers," Wiley, 2010, ISBN 978-0-470-87641-1.
3. Pain is a rational or emotional problem or desires the customer experiences.
4. David J. Bland and Alex Osterwalder, "Testing Business Ideas," Wiley, 2020, ISBN 978-1-119-55144-7.
5. Eric Ries, "The Lean Startup: How Constant Innovation Creates Radically Successful Businesses," Penguin UK, 2011, ISBN 978-0-670-92160-7.
6. Andy Rachleff on coining the term product-market fit, URL: https://open.spotify.com/episode/05NFnmgsjif5YDQeVGPfpz 2022-10-31, Last accessed 01-Oct-2022.
7. Marc Andreessen, "Part 4: The only thing that matters", Pmarchive, URL: https://pmarchive.com/guide_to_startups_part4.html, Last accessed 01-Oct-2022. Pmarchive is Marc Andreessen's blog with several useful insights for early-stage founders.
8. Nivi, "Steve Jobs does customer development, "09-Sep-2009, URL: https://venturehacks.com/jobs-customer-development: Last accessed 01-Oct-2022. This video clip of Steve Jobs also discusses this: https://www.youtube.com/watch?v=48j493tfO-o: last accessed 01-Oct-22.
9. Uday Phadke, Shailendra Vyakarnam, "Camels, Tigers & Unicorns," World Scientific, 2018, ISBN 978-1-786-34322-2, pp.27-29.

10. Uday Phadke & Sam Dods, "Idea to Impact Research Programme, Working Paper 1/Part 2: Maturity Mapping, May 2022, downloaded from https://www.thetriplechasm.com/research last accessed 03-Sep-22.
11. Uday Phadke and Shailendra Vyakarnam, "Scale-up Manual, The: Handbook For Innovators, Entrepreneurs, Teams And Firms," 1st Edition, Kindle Edition, World Scientific Publishing Europe Ltd., 2018,
12. Alison Olechowski, Steven D. Eppinger, and Nitin Joglekar, "Technology Readiness Levels at 40: A Study of the State-of-the-Art Use, Challenges, and Opportunities, 2015 Proceedings of PICMET '15, Management of the Technology Age, pp-2084-2094.
13. Kunal Shah, URL: https://www.linkedin.com/pulse/delta-4-theory-from-kunal-shah-sudharsan-d-r/: Last accessed 01-Oct-2022.
14. Roger L. Martin, "How to Prepare for Strategy: Less is More," URL: https://rogermartin.medium.com/how-to-prepare-for-strategy-4beaa4715c6e; Last accessed 12-Jul-2023.
15. Brian Halligan, "The Experience Disruptors," MIT Sloan Management Review, Vol. 61, No. 3, Spring 2020.

5

GOOD LOSS AND BAD LOSS

"Like many companies, we were always focused on our profit and loss statement. But cash flow was not a regularly discussed topic. It was as if we were driving along, watching only the speedometer, when in fact, we were running out of gas."

– *Michael Dell (1)*

YOU CAN DELEGATE ACCOUNTING, NOT FINANCE

Once upon a time, a small team of software experts working out of an apartment for a year developed a very innovative product. They pooled money from their friends and decided to take only a small salary to sustain themselves. Early customers loved their products. As the second year started, their buddy with marketing & sales experience joined the team. They had a great 2nd year selling their product and improving it, with a slight loss in their P&L statement. In the 3rd year, sales doubled, and they reported a small profit after tax as they concluded the 3rd year financial statements. They had an annual bash in a beach retreat and ordered T-shirts & coffee mugs for the whole team to remember the occasion. They believed investors had much interest in funding their firm. Pleasant meetings with analysts from venture capital firms. All of them wanted to keep in touch. Now they want to step up their salary a little bit. Alas, suddenly, they realize their firm can't serve more customers and is facing a shutdown in a couple of months due to "cash running out" unless they can find some funding very soon. The investors seem to take endlessly to decide. The outsourced accountant suggests laying off most employees to save on costs and statutory payments. What do they do now? Why do you think this could have happened?

DON'T START UP WITHOUT A GOOD CFO

In the initial months of most firms, they only make losses, as they have yet to be ready to sell anything. How do you know whether the loss you make is good or bad? Many founders are scared or ignorant of the financial aspects of the firm, especially when they have no previous exposure to finance, accounting, and compliance matters. This subject is usually not in the technologist or functional expert founder's comfort zone. Most founders fully outsource accounting and compliance to a professional services firm or even a freelance professional. That is appropriate to do. However, founders must learn finance and management accounting, pay attention to financial numbers, and realize that every decision anyone in the firm takes has financial consequences. Let us start understanding the domain of *financials*.

Financial Accounting, including taxation and compliance aspects, is an area that requires specialized qualifications and experience. It is best left to a *chartered accountant* (or, a certified public accountant) to handle. The financial accounting orientation is retrospective and compliant. The job of accounting is to record accurately what happened (economic transactions) and prepare financial statements according to the accounting principles (2) and the current regulatory frameworks of the region (state, country) the firm is operating. The question is: *"How did we get here?"*

Company Secretary is responsible for the efficient administration of a firm, particularly regarding ensuring compliance with statutory and regulatory requirements, managing the shareholding aspects, and ensuring that decisions of the Board of Directors are implemented. *A corporate lawyer* is concerned about the legal aspects of risk, terms of agreements established, intellectual property management, etc. These functions require specialized qualifications and experience.

Finance Management, on the other hand, is a business function concerned with investing the available financial resources for the best business results, economic aspects of the product and the market, and business projection based on strategic choices. In finance, the orientation is forward-looking. It constantly looks at the first principles that govern how we allocate capital to run the firm. It uses data from financial accounting. The guiding question is: *"What are our assumptions and choices about the future, and how shall we use the money we have?"* Every founder must learn the basics of financial management and appreciate its critical importance for the firm's viability, sustainability, and scalability. The founder must collaborate with a *trusted* financial advisor. This is often an external advisor with deep business experience or a virtual CFO firm that offers CFO services covering accounting, compliance, finance, and legal services. In this book, we shall refer to this position as a *good CFO*.

Neglecting the financial aspect of the firm will have dire consequences. Several startup firms fail due to poor cash management, bad resource use decisions, and bad terms of engagement with customers, investors, etc. It is not enough that you discover a good CFO; you must listen to them carefully and deliberate with them on the decisions you make. With the help of a good CFO, the founder must learn management finance and when and how to use the help from other professionals. As we saw in Chapter 1, running out of money is the number one situation for startup failures, and a good CFO will help you manage this risk. Founders must commit to investing their minds in developing this crucial competence as soon as possible. The learning curve to become a finance specialist, such as a *Chartered Financial Analyst*, is too steep. But, for the startup founder as a business leader, it is relatively easy to pick up. It requires critical thinking, school-level arithmetic skills, and exposure to a few standard patterns of finance management. This basic knowledge would help you determine when you need a specialist's help and seek it.

As a founder CEO, you must internalize the following terms as the first step: *asset, liability, (order) bookings, revenue, and profits, unit economics, direct and indirect costs/overheads, variable and fixed costs, capital expenses, debt and equity financing, gross and net margins/profits, operating profit/earnings, interest, tax, amortization, inventory, receivables, payables, break-even, cash flow positive, and pre-, and post-money valuation.* Essential concepts are *value, price, leverage, dilution, burn rate, customer lifetime value (LTV,) and customer acquisition costs (CAC.)* Founders need not be finance experts. But, as most decisions have financial implications, developing financial acumen will improve your ability to avoid catastrophic failures. It is about applying the filter of finance principles in every key decision, which implies *capital allocation*—financial and non-financial (founder's time, for instance, is the most expensive resource.) And it is about achieving growth (*return-on-investment*) than saving capital alone (or, *capital optimization.*)

A smart option for early-stage founders is to get a seasoned CFO as an Advisor to the firm, who can support the founder as and when needed. Internal CFO is a critical talent as part of the founding team if your firm plans to raise significant debt or equity capital. *Don't start without a clear, long-term CFO strategy.*

START WITH UNIT ECONOMICS

A simple *unit economics (UE)* modeling and analysis can help founders determine whether they are leading their firm to financial health or sickness. Many founders ignore this crucial business metric and doom their businesses. UE is the starting point for capturing your foresight and vision into economic value, which is vital in balancing the value creation (e.g., resource allocation) and value capture (e.g., pricing.)

In the early stages of a startup, most firms will be making financial losses, eroding the firm's capital. But how does the founder know whether such losses are *good or bad?* Is there a situation when *losing money is good?* Yes, when it is an investment for earning future income. For instance, in a DeepTech company, the initial years focus on building intellectual property assets that form the foundation for future moat and profits. Startups also invest in creating capability, growth, or building scale for future profitability. However, the scale will not create profits if there are fundamental flaws in the financial decisions or assumptions. UE or *contribution margin per unit* must be sufficient to absorb the operation costs as the unit volumes grow.

Unit Gross Margin (UGM) = Price (or revenue) per unit − Direct Costs per unit

Contribution Margin (CM) = Gross Margin − Indirect Costs per unit

From the above, we can conclude that only when the firm generates a positive CM increasing unit volume will result in profits. In other words, *economies of scale* will lead to profitability. You may feel this is something obvious to do. But the reality is that many startup firms need to do this analysis while fixing the pricing and direct cost of producing the unit revenue. There are multiple approaches to pricing the product or service. Founders must seek professional help earlier than later in determining the *pricing strategy*. This may point to approaches not related to the cost of creating the product but linked to the value the customer perceives or in the context of competitive alternatives. Careful analysis of UE is essential for DeepTech and high-growth DigitalTech ventures, which must invest heavily in creating assets, growing customer adoption, etc., that monetize later. It is about capturing value created through pricing.

UGM is a good indicator of *product/service innovation* in the solution delivered. When customers perceive a higher value received, they are willing to pay a higher price. On the other hand, innovative product designs optimize the direct costs as low as possible. As a result, product innovation is reflected in the UGM. CM is an indicator of *operational excellence* or optimizing the indirect costs or overheads.

How do we define *unit*? Picking the right unit to analyze is key to deriving insights about your firm's financial characteristics. At the most superficial level, a unit can be a unit of the product or service transaction. The unit can also be a Customer, an Operating Unit (e.g., a store,) a geographical location, or a combination of these. For multisided platforms, where multiple products/services are delivered with multiple revenue sources, UE is computed for each unit, as defined in the modeling. The Unit Economics model helps *triangulate* the different scenarios in a business model. For e.g., answer questions such as: "*How many bottles of juice must we be selling every day on average to break even?*" or "*How many active customers do we need to turn profitable?*"

Capture your assumptions and validate them about increasing the volume of sales. At what volume will you likely get a lower unit price from suppliers? Does your product roadmap plan increase value proposition, resulting in improved pricing later without increasing direct costs? Are there new revenue streams to become feasible later?

Unit economics assumptions are critical to validate in the real world to establish the firm's viability. Also, remember that UE analysis is only valid for a specific time, as the business environment continuously changes and influences the UE. Implementing certain aspects of UE analysis in software products/services is a smart way to accommodate the dynamics of the environment and receive alerts when necessary. Please refer to this article (3) for a detailed discussion with case studies about UE.

If your product satisfies the lower levels on Maslow's need hierarchy, you could expect larger number of customers and lower margins. Products satisfying higher level wants address fewer customers potentially at higher margins. This is a general principle applicable to utility products, but does not apply to "sin" situations—arms, addictive situations such as alcoholic beverages, games etc.

UNDERSTANDING DIRECT AND INDIRECT COSTS

In our modeling approach, direct costs apply to every unit sold. In other words, if there are no sales, the direct costs must drop to zero. In other words, direct costs are elastic with the revenue. For e.g., the materials cost for physical products or cloud hosting charges for software service will not be incurred if there are no sales.

Indirect costs are those costs that have no direct relation to unit sales. For example, rental for office facilities, marketing campaigns, or software development costs. The indirect costs can also be fixed or variable, so management can decide to make them elastic, but this does not happen automatically. Creating inventory in anticipation of future sales increases indirect cost. The goal in the initial days of the firm should be to keep the indirect costs as low and elastic as possible. As the firm grows, a good CFO can help manage the trade-off between fixed and variable costs.

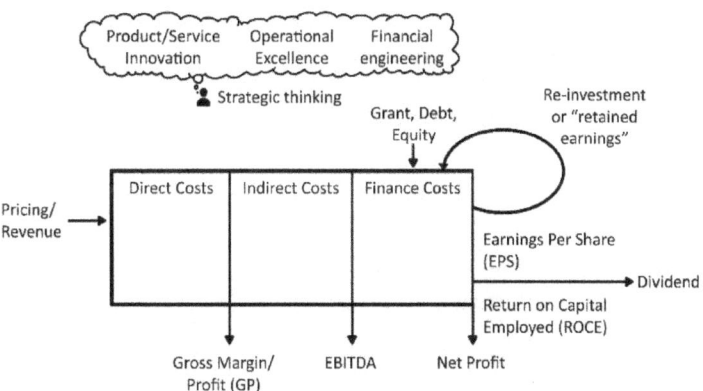

Visualize the firm as an engine that inputs revenue streams and produces earnings per share (EPS) as output. Imagine capital (equity, debt) to be the fuel to run the engine. The efficiency of the engine can be visualized as Return on Capital Employed, or RoCE. A well-designed business system must achieve highest possible RoCE. The figure helps visualize the business as a system with three distinct sections to focus on profitability. Founders must internalize this simple model to be able to relate the financial impact of management actions. Strategic thinking in startups must first focus on maximizing the Gross Profit with innovation. GP is what is available to sustain and operate the firm, and operational efficiency leads to a higher EBITDA for a given GP. Quality of the EBITDA, which represents the profitability from the operations, is an important factor to monitor. Revenue streams from any source that is not the core operations must be considered as "other income" and excluded in computing EBITDA. For instance, the founder and team might deliver training or consulting services as a source of additional cash to sustain the firm in its early days, which is not a long-term revenue stream of the firm.

STARTUP IS ABOUT CONVERTING CASH INTO ASSET

Cash and asset are two important concepts essential to internalize. Asset generates cash flows in the future. Cash in the firm is like breath. When the firm runs out of cash, it faces death and eventually dies. Cash flow statement is the most important financial statement to study carefully, especially in startups. This is the only financial statement meaningful to manage the startup. The startup process is to *maximize the conversion of the available cash efficiently and effectively into assets*, i.e., future cash. And protect your assets appropriately as you create them—be it competent people, process assets or inventions. DeepTech startups must learn clever ways to capture intellectual property (IP), secure incentives and allocate capital accordingly to protect IP assets. A well-articulated IP strategy and management process is perhaps the first management process to write in a DeepTech startup.

The Profit & Loss Statement and Balance Sheet does not have much relevance to manage in the early stages of a firm. These two statements when projected with assumptions, serve the purpose of helping decision making.

Imagine a technology-led startup firm to be an engine that

converts cash (capital) into assets initially such that the assets generate cash (revenue) in the future, ideally several multiples larger. When the firm generates substantial cash flows, as measured by *Free Cash flow to the Firm, or FCFF*, it reaches the **thriving state**. FCFF is the metric of a firm's profitability after all expenses and reinvestments to create assets.

SHOULD YOU RAISE VENTURE CAPITAL?

Once upon a time, a founder came out of a successful corporate career to launch a firm related to the digital convergence opportunity—computing, data communication, and consumer electronics. He, his cofounders, and a few angel investors pooled a decent amount of their hard-earned cash as seed money. The core team started the PoC development, and the founder spent most of his time developing an investment proposal and set out to raise 1M USD. Engaged an investment banker, met with numerous investors, and had detailed meetings with over twenty venture capital firms. After ten months, the capital was over, and the efforts to raise capital failed to deliver. The founder and core team had worked 24x7 for a year for the venture to eventually close.

The founder and team could have spent their time and money differently. What if they had optimized capital to discover and win a few early customers with pre-orders or advances? They could have generated customer revenue to fund their startup team and conserved capital to build assets. The firm would have survived if the founder had not diverted so much of his attention away from customers and building delivery capacity to raising venture capital.

Founders must carefully consider if they want to build a firm based on external venture capital or if it is feasible to bootstrap the firm. DeepTech and manufactured product ideas are generally unsuitable for bootstrapping, as they require significant capital to build the asset first before monetization. If you combine two or more ideas simultaneously with different monetization characteristics—say, subcontract engineering and product development—the firm's execution complexity increases and slows down or even dwarfs it. Use the projected cash flow statement to discover the capital requirements and whether the product sale can generate cash from revenue to build itself, and what the minimum capital is required to establish the viability of the idea.

Venture capital will be available only for business models that address an enormous market opportunity with growing profitability as revenue grows. Please note that this aspect has nothing to do with the firm or its founders. Once these two criteria are well established, the investors will be ready to assess the founder's capability to monetize the opportunity. Investors seek evidence in every step of their assessment.

PREPARE YOURSELF TO NEGOTIATE VALUATION

Any firm encapsulates assets. When you incorporate your company, you deposit money in the bank as *capital* to operate the business. Capital is needed to bridge the gap between the income from the operations of the business and the expenses. Let's say we started with 100 USD and issued 100 *equity shares* or common stock. The asset value or *economic value* or *valuation* of the company is 100 USD, and the *share price* is 1 USD. You own 100% of the firm.

Now you received investment from an external investor. Let us say you sold 100 shares for 2 USD each, receiving 200 USD. Now the firm's *pre-money valuation* is 100 USD, *post-money* valuation is 100+200 = 300 USD, and the total number of shares is 200. Post-money valuation is the firm's valuation *after* the additional capital is in the firm. Your ownership is *diluted* to 50%, and the investor's share of ownership is 50%. *Book value of the share is now 1.5 USD = 300 / 200.*

Note that the value of the share is now increased from 1 USD to 1.5 USD for you, and for the investor, it has been reduced from 2 USD to 1.5 USD. Then, why did the investor buy the shares at 2 USD? It is based on *intangible* assets that could cause *future income* for the firm and increase in the value of the firm, which is the element of *risk* in the investment. It is the investor's judgment in action deciding to invest. The investor trusts you and your ability to improve the firm's asset value much higher than 300 USD over time by executing a profitable operation. After one year, your firm produced 200 USD in net profits, meaning the *earnings per share* (EPS) is 1 USD. If you decide to retain the earnings in the firm, the valuation is now 300+200 = 500 USD, and the individual share value is 500/200 = 2.5 USD.

How can we determine a firm's value? As we saw earlier, it is based on *future results* that are highly unpredictable in the case of an early-stage startup. In the case of firms listed on the stock exchanges, there are several regulatory expectations for the firm. Further, the firm is beyond the *thriving stage* in the lifecycle curve and therefore is more *predictable*, or a *probability* can be attached to the estimations of future events. *Discounted Cash Flow (DCF)* is a legally acceptable method professional values use to estimate the value of established firms. The industry has accepted multiple sophisticated valuation methods—for instance, *cost-to-recreate*, *market-multiple*, etc. None of these apply to early-stage firms.

In the *idea stage*, the firm is only in the founder's imagination and the realm of *possibilities*. During the journey from idea to the thriving stage, the firm must be able to progressively improve the indicators to help estimate future events better or move to the realm of *plausibility*. In other words, someone who understands the business domain well can reasonably validate and estimate the *likelihood of the firm meeting its projections* based on its track record. The key takeaway for the founder here are:

- It is tough to get external professional investors to invest in a firm in the idea stage. Only friends, family, and others who perceive you as one of those ("Fs") will likely give you money.
- When you have made good progress in validating your hypothesis and building your product, you must create the information for the professional investors in *the language they*

can understand—verifiable facts, hypothesis, and numbers to be validated about the business model.

Most early-stage founders need to understand how investors *value* or assess startups. It is essential to develop a mindset about *startup valuation* if you are planning to raise equity funding from angel or venture investors. Let's start with a simple illustration. If your firm makes a net profit of 1M USD, and you have issued 1M equity shares, the earnings per share (EPS) is 1 USD. If an investor had purchased this share for 1 USD, the investment is returned in one year. The *firm's valuation* or *market capitalization* (4) is 1M USD, i.e., multiply the share price by the total number of shares. If the investor had paid 10 USD, it would take ten years to return the capital to the investor. This period translates as the Price / Earnings ratio, or PE ratio. Even in this case, the price is a considered judgment of the buyer, and there is no precise way to estimate it. For firms with a higher level of predictability of financial projections, several methods are accepted by the financial services industry to value a firm, e.g., Discounted Cash Flow (DCF.) Why would a firm earn a PE ratio above 40 years? The investor is willing to give a larger valuation because the investor believes that the firm will *increase its profitability* in the near future. In other words, *valuation recognizes the future profit potential or rate of increase of EPS*. If this cannot be established, even profit-making firms will not be worthy of venture investment at PE ratio (valuation.)

In the case of a startup with no or very low revenue, there is no way of analytically performing a valuation using industry-accepted methods such as DCF. The investor negotiates a *price for the share* with the founder (supported by existing investors and Advisors of the firm.) So, it is a *price discovery* process and not a scientific or analytical valuation.

WHAT IS THE MILEAGE OF YOUR VEHICLE

Imagine your firm to be powered by an engine (business system) that takes in revenue and converts to earnings. In addition, this engine could also influence the revenue, let's say. Its fuel is the capital, debt, and equity. The essential financial indicators of efficiency and effectiveness of the firm are:

1. Revenue growth
2. Profitability: Unit economics or gross margin per sale transaction and earnings per share.
3. FCFF, or free cash flow from the firm. This is the cash available for re-investing to scale up the firm or return as cash to investors. It is also known as *owner's cash flow*.
4. Rate of growth of net profit. This indicates how lucrative and scalable the business model is.
5. RoCE, or return on capital employed. This metric indicates how well your business model generates return for the capital invested (*capital efficiency*.) If you wanted a single measure of success of your firm, it is this one.

When you prepare the Rolling Forward Forecast, or RFF, these metrics must be projected. Regularly update the projections with actual performance metrics of the firm, and analyze the variances, positive or negative. It would help you fine tune your assumptions, goals and ultimately the business model (or, system) for better performance. And for you to design this vehicle, you must develop insights on designing the business model.

For most DeepTech, or manufacturing-oriented startups, what happens under the hood is really what the business is about. Direct customer adoption is away for by a few years (*gestation period*.) In such cases, the financial model of the outcome is what motivates the *right* investor to fund your firm. The challenge is to deliver quality product to the customers with minimum capital (capital optimization.) This is not about cutting corners. Digressing to other businesses may also divert your firm into a different destination.

Let's now get ready to jump over the widest chasm of all.

KEY TAKEAWAYS AND ACTION PLANNING

1. Develop your acumen in *corporate finance* and *behavioral finance*. Internalize the difference between finance and accounting.
2. Routinely watch for cash flow projections vs. actual and unit economics and establish targets and control limits.
3. Survival of the firm is the most important outcome of good execution, and depends on the cash position.
4. Internalize the difference between expenses and investments in asset building. Assets must deliver future revenue.
5. Get help from a *good CFO* (please see Appendix 1) early, as you achieve problem-solution fit and ready to move toward product-market fit.
6. Carefully consider the strategy to build your firm with or without venture capital, as early as possible, with a 5-7 year thinking horizon. Both approaches have crucial differences. *Under capitalization* also will stifle your startup.
7. The essential performance indicators of any startup venture are Revenue, Unit Economics, RoCE, FCFF and rate of growth of earnings.

CALL TO ACTION

1. For what value(s) are your customers genuinely willing to pay?
2. What is your plan to get the good CFO Service?
3. Prepare your unit economics and cash flow projections.
4. What are the assets of your firm—tangible and intangible—to generate future cash (revenue?)
5. Do you need capital to service customers' purchase orders or to build assets to sell in the future?
6. How much capital do you need to build assets, and validate your logical hypotheses?
7. Create your plan linked to the amounts of capital required

to produce outcomes and be flexible with outputs and timelines. For instance, "Get ten early customers sign up" is a good outcome to allocate capital for, compared to "Launch our website," which is an action and output entirely in our control.

8. How would you use the external capital to grow your firm's economic value—profitability and growth rate?
9. What business domain metric represents the survival risk of your firm? (e.g., % net profit much lower compared to the Enterprise Software industry benchmark, for a SaaS firm serving enterprises.)
10. Is your early loss good or bad? i.e., what portion of your capital are you converting into tangible or intangible assets that will generate revenue in the future?
11. Create a financial vision for your firm: Does your idea require a long gestation period and relatively significant capital to see the first customer purchase? Or can it hit a few customers quickly, but growing customers and revenue need capital and time?
12. Create the financial model projecting the metrics identified above. Use RFF process to continuously monitor the health of your firm. Once a quarter or sooner depending on the dynamics of the firm.
13. Review cash position, every day. Review cash flow statement weekly.

REFERENCES

1. Michael Dell, and Catherine Fredman: "Direct From Dell," Reprint Edition, 2010, Collins Business Essentials, HarperCollins. Kindle Edition. Pp. 47.
2. Please see https://www.investopedia.com/terms/g/gaap.asp to learn more about accounting principles.
3. Ramon Casadesus-Masanell, Dóra Horváth, and S. Ramakrishna Velamuri, "When Losing Money Is Strategic — and When It Isn't," MIT Sloan Management Review, February 22, 2022.
4. The term market capitalization or market cap is used in the context of firms listed on a stock exchange and traded among the public. In the context of startups and private companies use, the term is valuation.

6

JUMP OVER THE WIDEST CHASM

WHAT BUSINESS ARE WE IN?

Asim assembled a team of top-talent engineers, a few of them with the brain power of scientists. The R&D team came up with several inventions, innovations, and market-winner products that also won awards for the firm. They created many intellectual properties in different domains with global market relevance. The biggest challenge was determining which products/services to take to the market, which geographies, what channels, and what customer segments while operating with the parameters and constraints of the environment. The other dilemma was about how to deploy the inventions to the market—license it to a product company, or build a B2B business unit, or serve the end customers (B2C) delivering a service powered by the core invention? The questions were numerous; opinions and advice were plenty.

A few ideas succeeded in winning customer revenue profitably, while others could not find or sustain customer revenue for different reasons. Every idea showed different levels of adoption by early users. A few ideas required organizational capabilities that did not exist in the firm, learning different industry practices or combining with other innovations for practical use. It called for *strategic thinking*—deciding what to pursue, and what not to pursue—making tough choices.

Asim's challenge was designing *business models* around promising ideas and jumping over multiple chasms to maximize economic value creation. With a laser-sharp focus on value creation and a deep understanding of business models the firm could execute and scaleup, his firm's economic value grew phenomenally by unbelievable multiples, rarely seen in any industry globally.

ESSENTIALS OF BUSINESS MODELS

Chapter 4 introduced the essentials of value proposition and business model. In this chapter, we shall see more details on these critical topics founders must internalize. Remember, you start with a bunch of assumptions about value proposition and business model when you are at the CRL3 level. At this level, you must start defining the firm's value proposition and business model based on your hypotheses. If you persist and execute well, your firm could reach CRL10. As you progress through the levels, you will validate or invalidate your assumptions, do pivots, and continue refining the business model supported by validated hypotheses (i.e., facts and data.) In this journey, crossing Chasm II, or the transition from CRL6 to CRL7, has several aspects of the business model to be proven with evidence from the market. We shall see a few aspects of this in this Chapter.

Alexander Osterwalder (2) originated the *business model canvas* and defined the *business model* as follows: *A business model describes the rationale of how an organization creates, delivers, and captures value.* We shall adopt the definition in this book with a minor modification.

"*A business model describes the rationale of how an organization creates, delivers, and captures value in the context of the ecosystem and environment in which it operates.*"

This definition includes the importance of monitoring the ecosystem and environment to rapidly respond to the changes around the business model canvas elements.

VALUE IS IN THE EYES OF THE BEHOLDER

Your decision to plunge into a venture into a business starts with an *idea* that solves a problem a human being suffers. This idea must be developed into a *value proposition* in the beneficiary or customer's words. We realize that customers don't buy products but solutions to their problems, alleviate their pains (needs), or fulfill their desires (wants.) They are buying to change their emotional state, which is an emotionally driven decision. Value proposition answers your *ICP's question*: "*why should I buy what you sell, from you?*" The value proposition must be articulated in words that customers can relate to and resonate with. At this stage, you are ready to create the *Customer Pitch*, which is the first external communication of the startup—in the form of a presentation, website, etc. The *number of customers* is the primary metric to indicate the firm's growth on its lifecycle trajectory.

A few foundational concepts must be internalized in understanding *economic value* or *value*. The Customer has a specific *upper limit* of money she is willing to exchange for the product/service. As the product provider, your firm has a specific *lower limit* of money you are willing to exchange the product for. If your price, typically higher than your firm's lower limit, is lower than the Customer's upper limit, customers perceive value in buying. Similarly, as a "buyer," your firm has similar exchange considerations for its consumption to produce the product/service—materials, people, services, and so on. If the price your firm is willing to pay is higher than the *willingness to sell* limit, your firm will succeed in acquiring the resources it needs. The difference between the price and cost is the profit, or value your firm can retain as profit.

Now, to maximize the profit for the firm, the firm must achieve the maximum possible price and minimum possible cost. In other words, the firm must communicate its benefits to the customers, employees, and suppliers to reduce the gaps. Maslow's hierarchy of needs (3) presents a robust framework for understanding *needs* and *wants*. Based on this framework, we can understand that when our product/services address the lower levels of the hierarchy pyramid, there will be an easier PSF. However, there would also be several competitors who could address that need, and as a result, the firm is likely to see resistance to earning higher profits. To be viable, such firms will require a higher volume of units to be sold.

On the other hand, it is harder to serve the emotional and social needs, as it gets very diverse and personal. Serving customers in this space would offer you greater profit opportunities in a lower volume. As an example, think about *personal mobility* as a fundamental problem being solved. Vehicles for the masses struggle to get higher prices even though they serve many customers. On the other hand, luxury vehicles can earn a much higher price on a significantly low volume. This establishes the need to *design your product around the pricing*. Innovative products that address the lower and higher levels of Maslow's hierarchy can generate exponentially growing profits only when the product design and business model are aligned. Ideas that aim to deliver public good are, therefore, more complex to establish viability and sustainability even though the need is not questionable. For instance, a device to aid blind people that they cannot afford to buy.

When customers cannot afford, they may accept being at the lowest level of the hierarchy and would be willing to suffer a poorer experience while consuming the product. When customers have the affordability, they start moving up the hierarchy and will be willing to pay for *customer experience*. Consider a cup of coffee sold by a street vendor versus Starbucks versus in a five star restaurant to appreciate the value of customer experience. This is an essential ingredient in designing your value proposition.

There are several patterns of value propositions. Consider three value propositions that could be mapped to your product: "*I will help you make money,*" "*I will help you save money/time,*" and "*I will keep you out of trouble,"* You can understand that it would be progressively tricky to realize value from the customer. On the other hand, *"I will take you out of trouble"* would be valued highly. The *Oxygen, Aspirin, Jewelry analogy* (4) is an excellent way to think about value proposition design. Oxygen is an absolute need; aspirin is a painkiller, and jewelry is a luxury.

It is best to articulate the value in the customer's context and language. The only way you will learn how to do this is through numerous customer discovery interviews you do. It takes careful effort to create a compelling value proposition communication about your product/service to grow your customer base beyond proto- and charter customers.

KNOW YOUR CUSTOMER, ONCE AGAIN

Advances in science pave the way for the invention of new technology. The new technology builds a new capability, and new products emerge based on the new technology. The new products are integrated with other products as *a system of interacting components* to benefit the end-users or *people*. Economic value is exchanged for the benefits people receive. The figure shows the stack of a technology business with associated risks to be managed for effective benefits delivery. A newly configured stack can disrupt the existing value chains as the user is concerned only about the benefits or jobs to be done. This happens when new disruptive business models bypass existing value chains and associated incumbent firms. Such full-stack DeepTech businesses create quicker diffusion of innovation and greater economic value for the originator of the technology. For instance, if Tesla were to operate as an automotive component supplier to established automotive companies, it might not have created the disruption and associated economic value.

We often see multiple market opportunities for the technology solution we have developed (e.g., an AR/VR platform applicable to education, product maintenance, healthcare, etc.) We can't go after all the opportunities simultaneously, as we are small and don't have the resources. It is an essential strategic question that the founder must first answer before venturing to monetize their innovation. Inventors of new technologies valuable to one or more industries could license the technology to the industry players. This is a good approach for universities and scientific research labs, whose primary goal is to advance scientific knowledge and technology development. At the next level, a founder could limit their play to any step in the stack. Their customers will be in the next step of value addition before the technology delivers benefits to the end-user.

	People	Consumption Risk
Distribution Professional services	Benefits Delivery	Execution Risk
Outsourcing Contract/ gig economy	Products	Market Risk
Open innovation Academic/ sponsored research	Technology Science	Technology Risk
Labor Arbitrage Models	Economic Value Creation (Innovation value chain)	Business Risk Management

In the full stack DeepTech approach, the firm directly delivers the benefits to the end user. It is more intimidating, capital intensive, and challenging to execute, as it must overcome all the risks—technology, market, execution (scaling), and consumption risks. And ultimately, it transforms the original industry into a new technology-based industry and delivers improved benefits and customer experience to the end-users.

The advantage of the full-stack approach is the large total addressable market powered by the capability (e.g., lower cost, reduced complexity.) It also enables speed and control of the value chain, directly interfacing with the end consumer of the benefit. It creates opportunities to address adjacent market opportunities more easily (e.g., Tesla launching solar roof.) The *market space* addressed due to the new full-stack DeepTech firm can look very different from the existing market space it disrupted. It is also more capital efficient ultimately.

The downside of the approach is the complexity and complicatedness inherent to creating and managing the full-stack service (benefit delivery.) It calls for higher capital in the early stages of the business, typically before it reaches the thriving stage, and a diverse, interdependent leadership to execute the business model. It is inherently harder to execute for the technologist founder. But, the hardness of execution can reward the founder heavily when successful, creating a natural moat against the competition.

The *cost arbitrage models* serve the full-stack value chain players by providing a commodity to expert-level talent-based *professional services* or *contract manufacturing* services. They contribute value to the main full-stack players as more efficient and less risky options for the resources they require to augment owned resources.

In the overall market space, the startup firm must strategically choose to position itself as per its realities and capabilities. This choice need not be a permanent position. It can navigate itself into different positions as the firm generates profit. It is also the choice of the founder and partners how that profit will be used: re-invest to scale (building capabilities) at considerable risk or take out of the firm as fruits of their labor. Based on this choice, the definition of the customer changes and brings associated complexities that must be managed.

For instance, if your firm has Deep Technical capabilities and innovation in a specific technical domain, let's say artificial intelligence (AI,) the firm must make the strategic choice of where to position in the value chain. For instance, they can create a food delivery service (vertical) using AI and develop the business model in the benefits delivery layer or be an AI professional services firm that provides product engineering services to a digital-tech firms (horizontal.) While the technical team's AI innovation capabilities are the same, the customers and the problem they solve for those customers are dramatically different. To succeed as a food-delivery firm, it must understand and serve the consumers for their needs and wants by expanding the firm's capabilities far beyond engineering AI products. After succeeding in achieving a thriving state, the firm could either vertically dive deeper to develop a full-stack business model or horizontally serve another consumer niche, say flowers or medicine delivery. *"Where to play in a market space"* is an important strategic decision.

CUSTOMER PITCH IS YOUR MOST IMPORTANT PITCH

The solution need not be built out completely for making the customer pitch. The customer pitch's objective is to find the fit between the solution and the corresponding problems the customers suffer or their JTBD. Even when starting with a research commercialization or an initial product prototype, it is essential not to be too attached to the product. Instead, get attached to the customers and their problems. Consequently, you may get the question, *"Can I build it?"* rather than *"does someone need it?"* Solutions to such problems arise from real customer needs, resulting in patents with greater commercial value. Customers resonating with your solution pitch is a good indicator of what to build in your product, making your journey to PMF easier. Continuously improve your customer pitch as you refine the business model. And sharpen your listening skills as you meet more customers.

When your idea meets Customers, it will change. You must be willing to iterate your idea several times with customer feedback. A firm that is not quickly ideating, rapidly learning from the customers, and changing assumptions is not moving fast enough. This process is known as *pivoting*. Pivoting helps optimize opportunity cost and gain from new alternatives compared to the currently chosen ones. Pivoting must be done with careful consideration.

How shall you not introduce your firm? Certainly not as a *"SaaS company"* or *"Blockchain Startup."* Please introduce yourself in the way the customer should say about your product or firm to their friend or colleague in their context.

What shall not be used in a value proposition? One of the significant challenges for a subject matter expert in formulating and articulating the value proposition is the feeling of *obviousness* or *self-evidence* of the solution. This shows up as technical terms (e.g., virtualized service layer) and acronyms (e.g., OFDM) of your industry in the value proposition statement. Empty words that describe value proposition in a non-tangible way must be eliminated, too (e.g., disruptive, exceptional, low-cost.) Your ICP must feel the power of your solution.

SHALL WE FISH IN THE POND OR SAIL THE DEEP SEA

According to Bill Gross, who has incubated numerous ideas into business ventures, *timing* is the most prominent reason startups succeed (5). The crux of go-to-market strategy is to crack the complexity of timing for the right customer, at the right place, and the right price. The timing factor is linked closely to the customer experience that can be effectively delivered with the maturity level of technology. As technology maturation cycles are hard to predict, getting the timing right often is a matter of *serendipity*—but it can be a planned luck.

The essential considerations of Go-to-Market (GtM) strategy are based on the realities and resources you can muster: how big is the customer segment, is the segment willing and able to pay, do we have easy access to them, how long would it take to win commercial orders from this customer, etc. Firms can create a unique competitive advantage by creating valuable intellectual property assets engaging with the proto, charter, and earlier adopters of mainstream customers.

HOW TO CATCH ELEPHANTS?

Many founders do not fully comprehend the difference between *growing* and *scaling up* the firm. When many founders say, "we want to scale up," or "we scaled up in the last year," they often mean growth. Growth is about growing business, or external results. Typical growth measures are the number of customers, revenue, profits, customer satisfaction, etc. While savvy founders would pay attention to the growth of profits as revenue grows, many founders are satisfied by profits growing linearly or less than linearly with revenues. When the firm's business model can deliver exponentially increasing net profit as the revenue increases, it is a highly *scalable* business model. *Scalability* is a property architected into the business model in the different components of the firm. Scalability is the property of the business model that delivers *economies of scale*. Scaling up the firm is about internal actions to build capability and productivity that delivers corresponding growth characteristics. *PMF is a pre-condition for scaling up.*

The conventional growth approach is to operate efficiently, optimize capital, and remove the risks and uncertainties in the business model. As certainty improves, as PMF indicates, the firm is ready to scale... This is the classic approach to *scaling up* or non-linearly increasing net profits in relation to the revenue increase. Firms with solid differentiation have unique inventions that enable an advanced product, unique customer experience, or a unique manufacturing process. DeepTech or DigitalTech firms initially work with the proto- and charter customers to achieve the PMF. After that, the firm can *fastscale* the business by deploying external capital and rapidly growing its customer base into mainstream customers. The fundamental pre-condition for fastscaling the firm is

PMF with attractive *unit economics* that is possible for firms with strong competitive advantage (or business moat.) Typical moats for DeepTech firms are lack of direct competition in the near term, intellectual property assets such as patents and trade secrets. DigitalTech firms, on the other hand, benefit from *network effects* (the value of a product or service grows as its user base expands) and *switching costs* (e.g., customers lock in a specific cloud service due to the difficulties of moving data to an alternative service.) Economies of scale and lower cost of production due to efficient supply chain can emerge as moats as the firm grows to grab a leading market share.

Blitzscaling (6) is a set of tactics and strategy for *growing* a business rapidly by prioritizing speed over efficiencies, even in an environment of uncertainty. Blitzscaling is inherently a higher-risk strategy, harder to execute, calls for more considerable capital, and can result in a catastrophic failure of the firm if the mainstream customer adoption does not happen. Remember, blitzscaling aims to achieve phenomenal growth despite increased costs and losses and achieve remarkable outcomes (i.e., growing profits) following that phase. This approach makes sense only when the speed of customer acquisition is a critical element of your business model. Many internet and DigitalTech firms, such as Amazon and Airbnb, have pioneered and succeeded in blitzscaling their firms after the "dot-com" decade. The characteristics of the DigitalTech business models particularly fit well with the blitzscaling approach. Founders embarking on such business ideas must establish evidence early in their journey that their firm has an enormous market opportunity to be grabbed rapidly and can build their moat with network effects and more extensive customer adoption. If their firm mixes in technology innovation to deliver unique customer experience and value (i.e., intellectual property), it can be more attractive to early-stage investors to invest in. Blitzscaling assumes a huge market space opportunity.

Every firm aspires to sustain growth in customers, revenue, people, geographies, etc. *Scalability* indicates the capability of the firm to execute this aspiration. It indicates the preparedness of a firm to proliferate, whether it can handle sustained periods of growth with minimal disruption to the quality and without increasing the risk. Scalability exists in the foundation and infrastructure of the firm—leadership talent, the technical architecture of the product, its production, delivery functions (systems & processes,) onboarding customers (experience, support), and so on. Growth is related to scalability and is dependent on it.

Scalability must be designed early in the life of the firm. The business model canvas covers scalability through Key Activities, Key Resources, and Key Partnerships. Introduce metrics early in these areas for establishing scalability. Always think and operate as if you are already at the level you want to be in the next 2-3 years. Where would your firm break if your revenue doubled or tripled in the next quarter/year? Can you deliver if you just received an investment, and your investors want you to grow revenue rapidly? What is the relationship between your revenue and profit growth? Is your firm (and its business model) capable of delivering a higher profit growth rate as revenue grows?

Scalability is not easy to design in the business model and execute. It also calls for increased risk-taking ability. When it takes a lot of resources (capital or people) to sustain and grow results, the business model is not considered highly scalable and cannot easily increase the number of customers (e.g., consulting, advertising, accounting, or law firms.) Therefore, many successful entrepreneurs stabilize their firms as MSMEs and produce relatively stable results and stagnate. They add relatively low economic value compared to firms that scaleup in the same industry. A startup, in our definition, is not a small version of the mature company. Startup aspires to scaleup and achieve a dominant position in a chosen market space.

Venture Capitalists (VC) look for the rapid growth of economic value in 3-7 years. Only certain kinds of startup firms are appropriate to produce the kind of results VCs want. A startup firm is *scalable* when its business model yields a rate of increase in profitability (ΔEPS, ΔROCE) higher than the rate of increase in revenue

(ΔRevenue.) *Scalability* indicates how big the firm's economic value could grow. Such a projection elicits interest from investors if a plausible narrative supports the financial projections.

Subroto Bagchi's thought-provoking book (7) on embracing scale early is a good resource for first-time founders who want to develop a deeper understanding of the scaling challenge. Learn the patterns of business models and adopt and adapt what works best for your reality—experiments with the real world is the only way to build evidence and, ultimately, economic value in the firm. Alexander et al. capture several thought-provoking business model patterns (8). Another source for business model patterns is *Business Model Navigator* (9).

A startup firm is an extreme leadership challenge to drive change—externally and internally. *Systems thinking* is an essential competency to develop for founders and founding teams. We can observe systems at different levels—product, in its adoption as part of the customer's context, the firm, and its existence in the ecosystem and environment. Systems thinking is about understanding the forces and interrelationships that shape the behavior of a system. Startup firms must be *rapid learning organizations*. This discipline helps us to change systems more effectively and act more in tune with the natural process of the world (10).

You may have a great product design, which does not necessarily mean a good business design. Remember, you are building a firm, not a product. What do you do when you are building your product? You will insert probes at appropriate places to measure how your product is coming together, isn't it? It is time to learn how to insert probes into your firm. Let's go!

KEY TAKEAWAYS AND ACTION PLANNING

1. A business model describes the rationale of how an organization creates, delivers, and captures value in the context of the ecosystem and environment in which it operates—in simple terms, *how do you make money to sustain*

and scale?

2. The business model evolves in the mind of the founder and team, starting as a bunch of assumptions. The firm validates, changes and establishes evidence and facts over time.
3. Customers confirm the product's value in their context and language.
4. Careful consideration is necessary to design the business model based on a technology breakthrough—a full-stack firm serving the consumer (B2C or D2C) or a component supplier serving many firms (B2B) that serve different categories of consumers.
5. Customer pitch is the first presentation to prepare and refine.
6. Growth is about external results, or outcomes. Expansion is about increasing capacity and reach. Scaling is about building capability and productivity in the business model to achieve economies of scale and aspire to win a substantial part of the market space the firm serves.
7. Systems thinking is essential for designing effective business models.

CALL TO ACTION

1. Develop your customer pitch and improve it with customer feedback—use the customer's context and language.
2. Learn to use tools such as Value Proposition Canvas, Business Model Canvas, Business Model Navigator, and Triple Chasm tools (or their equivalent methods) that help you systematically develop and manage your business model.
3. Develop the *pricing strategy*, which is the way to establish the value of your product or service. Pricing based on customer value rather than a cost-plus approach is critical in the early stages of DeepTech startups. Even when the product idea is about lower price, the firm cannot sustain without

significantly lower cost due to innovation.

4. Develop your *go-to-market strategy*, analyzing your firm's capabilities and resources and maximizing the profitability in a niche to establish early customer adoption and reinforcing your moat in the customer's context.
5. Build systems thinking as a competency to shape your firm as a learning organization.

REFERENCES

1. Giff Constable, "Talking to Humans: Success starts with understanding your customers," 1st edition, Amazon Kindle Edition, 2014, ISBN 978-0-9908009-1.
2. Alexander Osterwalder and Yves Pigneur, "Business Model Generation: A Handbook for Visionaries, Game Changers, and Challengers," (p. 14), 2010, Wiley. Kindle Edition.
3. Saul McLeod, "Maslow's Hierarchy of Needs," Simply Psychology, last updated, 04-Apr-2022, Retrieved: 01-Oct-2022. This article discusses the topic in simple language and in sufficient detail.
4. Ilan Mochari, "A 10-Second Method to Test the Vitality of Your Startup Idea," Inc., May 9, 2014, https://www.inc.com/ilan-mochari/janet-krauss-how-to-test-the-vitality-of-your-startup-idea.html: Last accessed 31-Oct-2022.
5. Bill Gross TED talk on "The single biggest reason why start-ups succeed" https://www.youtube.com/watch?v=bNpx7gpSqbY accessed on 20-Jan-2022. This TED talk by Bill Gross has over five million views, and it is a must-watch for tech founders.
6. Reid Hoffman and Chris Yen, "Blitzscaling: The Lightning-fast Path to Building Massively Valuable Companies," 2018, Currency New York, ISBN 978-1-5247-6141-7: A pioneering book that describes the Blitzscaling in detail.
7. Subroto Bagchi, "The Elephant Catchers: Key Lessons for Breakthrough Growth," Hachette India, 2017, ISBN 978-9-351-95000-4.
8. Alexander Osterwalder, Yves Pigneur, Alan Smith, and Frederic Etiemble, "The Invincible Company: How to

Constantly Reinvent Your Organization with Inspiration From the World's Best Business Models," Wiley, 2020, ISBN 978-1-119-52396-3. A seminal work on capturing contemporary business models; a good reference book for founders exploring business model options.

9. Oliver Gassmann, Karolin Frankenberger, and Michaela Csik, "Business Model Navigator," FT Publishing International, 2014, Amazon Kindle Edition, Companion URL: https://businessmodelnavigator.com/explore: Last accessed on 01-Oct-2022.

10. Peter M. Senge, "The Fifth Discipline: The art and practice of the learning organization," Second edition, Cornerstone Digital, 2010, Amazon Kindle Edition. A classic book on systems thinking in the business context and learning organizations.

7

ILLUMINATE YOUR FIRM

"In the beginning, when God created the universe, the earth was formless and desolate. The raging ocean that covered everything was engulfed in total darkness, and the Spirit of God was moving over the water. Then God commanded, "Let there be light,"—and light appeared. God was pleased with what he saw. Then he separated the light from the darkness, and he named the light "Day" and the darkness 'Night.' The evening passed, and morning came—that was the first day."

– The Book of Genesis.

PLAYING THE NUMBER GAME

By age twenty-five, life appeared to be pre-planned for Asim. He inherited his family's positive values and a thriving, traditional business after his education at a best-in-class university his father could afford to send him to. As he started a leadership position in the firm, he was a keen observer and a curious learner. He received positive, encouraging answers when he asked anyone how the firm was doing. Asim's grandfather had established the firm, and his father had helped him grow the firm to a thriving level with loyal employees and customers. They had learned from their business experience and through ups and downs. The firm was running well as far as profits were concerned. Asim was uncomfortable, however. He perceived possibilities for profits to rise. He thought the firm might not sustain conventional working methods with emerging business and digital economy models in the modern world. He felt uncomfortable that he could not determine how the firm was *really* doing. He started to get comfortable being uncomfortable and started to question more. He started seeking facts and numbers in reporting and proposal presentations. Asim followed what God did—he created light first and separated the day and night. The firm moved from general answers and anecdotes to specific numbers, and facts that can be tracked. This cultural change quickly scaled to implement digital solutions leveraging analytics techniques. Profits grew, and there was more free cash flow to invest in new business initiatives. Those also run based on evidence-based, facts-based reviews providing operational autonomy with financial and operational accountability, and *customer experience driving the decisions.* The outcomes for the firm turned dramatically superior and produced exceptional economic value.

GOOD STRATEGY, BAD STRATEGY

Let us develop a simple common understanding of what has come to be known in the industry as *"strategy."* First, why do we need a strategy? What would guide our decision-making when we all, including the founder/CEO, are busy with day-to-day actions? It is impossible to consult and get a consensus about every decision. The strategy provides the context and guiding principles for individuals to operate, aligned with a larger goal. The term originated in military circumstances, where life depends on autonomous actions guided by pre-determined guidance or *strategy*.

It begins with discovering the critical factors (*"the current state"*) resulting from a *diagnosis*. Following this, define a reasonable definition of the situation your firm wants to reach (*"the destination state"*). Strategy is about *how* your firm will move forward, design the path, make choices, and align actions, people, and resources to reach the destination. A good strategy must honestly acknowledge the challenges and provide an approach to overcome them. Michael Porter states, *"The essence of strategy is choosing what not to do."* The most basic idea of strategy is the application of strength against weakness. Or strength applied to the *most promising* opportunity and win against the competing alternatives. And the best strategy is to avoid a war—create a unique position where three is no competition. Strategy is based a set of hypothesis. Its ultimate worth is determined by its success (1). The founder/CEO is accountable for developing and communicating the strategy. Influential founders do this collectively with their teams.

Strategy is about explaining how you would secure your firm's economic prosperity, the logic by which the firm gets enough resources to survive and thrive. *Planning* is about the order of execution or the sequence of actions you and the team will do. Knowing *why* you have a reason to do those actions and *what the outcomes* will be is essential for effective execution. Strategy requires you to interact with the people and entities outside your firm. So strategy must be dynamic, as you don't have complete control over them. You have full control over your action plan, but it must also be dynamic as it follows the strategy. *The plan is the tactics to execute the strategy.*

Strategy is about outcomes we are seeking. Planning is about internal actions and allocation of resources (capital) we propose to use to produce outputs. Therefore, planning is relatively easy, and strategy is harder. Many founders don't internalize this difference, and struggle to create and communicate effective strategy for the firm.

Marketspace analysis and size estimates are *essential to* developing the firm's strategy. We must understand how the customer is solving their problem now and how our idea will change how they do it, creating a *customer-centric value chain*. Who are the key players in the space now, and how are they fulfilling their role in the *value chain* of delivering the solution to the *ultimate end-user* of the value? Where are we proposing to play in this value chain? Is it likely that the value chain itself would change as a result? Can we deliver additional value to the same customer by partnering with others? For instance, can you offer insurance or deferred payment options along with your product, which may be serviced by partnering financial institutions? Can we own and operate our product and only deliver the value to the customers on a *pay-as-you-use* basis? This strategy and business model is *servitization* (2), requiring a carefully developed financial strategy to execute well.

A PESTEL analysis is a strategic framework commonly used to evaluate the business environment in which a firm operates. Traditionally, the framework was referred to as PEST analysis, an acronym for Political, Economic, Social, and Technological; in recent history, the framework was extended to include Environmental and Legal factors.

MEASURE WHAT MATTERS: As you build your product and the firm, you must gather data and evidence to know whether you are progressing. Establishing quantitative measures for the product and the critical business processes that significantly impact your firm's progress would be best.

Let's face it, many founders are not number-oriented, and they prefer to live in an *intuitive and qualitative* world. If you are one such founder, please collaborate with a co-founder, team member, or external consultant who can support you in establishing the *appropriate* measurement system as you progress. It is never too early to think about metrics to create accurate visibility to progress.

In the early days of your firm, most of the firm will be in *discovery mode*, running experiments or testing the market. While you must look for evidence and data *after* the discovery mode, *during* the discovery mode, it may not be feasible to establish quantitative measures for the process (other than those which are part of the experiment or hypothesis testing itself.) Where there are stable processes, metrics can be established, and the process can be managed using *performance indicators*. Processes must have *lead (what we can measure early)* and *lag (what we can measure only at the end)* indicators. Similarly, the measures must distinguish between *outputs (our deliverables)* and *outcomes (results of interaction with the stakeholders.)* For instance, the outcome of a digital marketing campaign is *qualified leads* that can convert to customers. Launching the campaign is an output. Incoming customer contacts are the outcome and a leading indicator. The outcome is the number of customers who signed up and the *conversion rate* from leads to customers indicate the effectiveness.

As the firm matures, the number of processes and metrics grows exponentially. So, when the business processes stabilize and enter *maintenance/sustenance mode*, we regularly monitor only the key performance indicators (KPIs)—for instance, Order Bookings. We also establish *control limits* for individual processes to *trigger exceptions* when a process is out of control. Creating a quantitative management culture in the firm lays the foundation for scalability. Use KPIs for all processes in the maintenance mode—these are like the instrument panel of your car to know about its condition.

In the early stages of your firm, we want to know how we are progressing toward our goals. *Objectives and Key Results (OKRs)* is a founder/CEO's tool for *driving focus, alignment, and engagement* in the firm. OKRs is *a critical thinking framework and ongoing discipline that seeks to ensure that employees work together, focusing effort to make measurable contributions* (3). It is never too early to use OKRs in your firm.

The *objective* is your destination—*what* is to be achieved. Objectives are qualitative, significant, and inspiring. Usually, OKRs are defined for 2 or 4 months, a year, or three years. The *Key Results* are markers of your progress—*how* are you progressing? They are quantitative outcomes that are *specific, measurable, achievable (with a stretch,) realistic, and implicitly time-bound (to the OKRs cycle), or SMART.*

If your team size includes full-time and all other contributors, such as consultants and advisors, OKRs can make a huge difference in your strategic execution. OKRs complement KPIs—like your GPS navigator and your car's windshield complement your vehicle's dashboard meters. OKRs help you know your progress toward your destination, while KPIs support troubleshooting and making your system efficient. Don't try to scale up without OKRs.

Developing an *outcome mindset* over the output (deliverables) obsession is essential, along with using OKRs. *An outcome is a change in human behavior that drives business results* (4). Outcomes are consequences of behavior or action by someone other than you (and your firm)—customers, users, or employees. For instance, launching your product is output. Users using the product and customers paying for it are outcomes.

VISUALIZE YOUR FIRM AS AN ENGINE

Introduce a vital Rolling Forward Forecast (RFF) process in your firm that you can use to checkpoint the venture monthly or quarterly in the initial quarters. It is a forecasting process wherein you imagine or try to forecast your cash outflows, inflows, revenues, etc., monthly for the next 12 months and quarterly for two years. The RFF process must cover all the critical metrics for your firm. The RFF process covers all revenue streams and cost structure metrics in the business model canvas.

After executing for one month, post the actuals ("what happened?") and repeat the projection. In the initial quarter, the ability to forecast will be low, and the variance will be high. The purpose is to interrogate the variance and learn from it. Progressively, with experience, the variances would reduce in certain areas starting with costs, and predictability will improve. This discipline set in the firm would help the team manage the challenging times well with information visibility in advance.

It requires help from a well-qualified finance professional. This process is termed *financial modeling*, which starts with the unit economics model, projects revenue and costs, and projects the cash flow statement, income (profit-and-loss) statement, and balance sheet. It is a simulation of the business using future financial numbers, linking them to your firm's business model narrative—your assumptions and your strategic choices. The strategic choices will reflect cost assumptions and expectations of outcomes linked to those costs or investments. It is practice to model your finances every quarter as you discover your market space, develop your business model, and validate your hypotheses.

In the case of new ventures, the cash flow and cost management assume more importance in the early stages of planning and tracking to validate the assumptions about the venture. The projections must be revised at least quarterly or as and when there is significant learning. In the early stages of the venture, make it a practice to project (estimate) the next twelve months monthly and the eight quarters to follow. *Thousand days* as a horizon to achieve significant milestones, and attempting to create visibility for that period is reasonably achievable with practice/experience over time. The accuracy of projections is less important than knowing why the variance happened and whether key assumptions were validated or invalidated. Progressively accuracy will improve first for the costs and then for the revenue. You can expect a high accuracy of projections only as you approach the *thriving state*, well past PMF and CRL10.

Establishing the RFF process will naturally help the capital-raising efforts in the future. The founder would become comfortable linking the product vision narrative and numbers well and can answer the questions on variances well. In an early venture, linking milestones to capital allocation is more helpful than to timelines. Achieving a certain milestone schedule such as a "product launch" is more for internal pride than of any consequence. Schedules assume greater importance, when these are committed to customers and linked to customer's plans.

Your product innovation initiatives have a direct relation to the Gross Profit. As a result of innovation, the product would be more valuable to the customer (yield better pricing) or reduce the direct costs of delivering the solution. Innovative ventures aim to maximize the firm's gross profit, which is the cash the firm earns to support itself. Gross profit pays for the firm's overheads (or indirect costs), leading to the EBITDA. The efforts on operational excellence must improve the ratio of EBITDA to Gross Profit. What follows EBITDA to the firm's net profit and earnings per share are in the parlance of the finance and accounting professionals. This is the area where a good CFO's advice is invaluable. The most important metric is the Return on Capital Employed (ROCE), which includes the total capital and debt deployed to produce the returns.

RESPECT THE KING AND STAND UPSIDE DOWN

Even after growing their firms' revenues, many founders struggle with the concept of profit vs. cash. Understanding that difference is critical to understanding how cash flow works in the firm. Mastering the practice of proper cash flow management for the firm can mean the difference between failure and success. This is the best place to start developing your finance management competence. Cash is the *king* of any firm, and always respect this king.

After the cash flow, the Income Statement or Profit-and-Loss Statement is the following vital statement. Rita Gunther McGrath and Ian C. MacMillan introduced *Discovery-Driven Planning* (DDP) in their Harvard Business Review paper in 1995 as the new way to plan financials for new ventures (5). Following this, more details are published about this powerful technique for planning new ventures (6) (7). The *reverse income statement* way of planning is consistent with the approach of new ventures to start with hypotheses and validate them. Instead of estimating the venture's revenue first and applying costs to derive the profit or loss, the reverse income statement starts with the *profit target* to make the venture worthwhile. The steps in discovery-driven planning are:

1. Start with the profitability target in the plan.
2. Identify all the required and allowable costs to produce,

deliver and service the product.
3. Estimate the revenue required to make the venture worthwhile, as per #1 above.
4. Identify your assumptions—hypotheses that must be validated.
5. Establish if the venture can be viable.
6. Validate the hypotheses at defined milestones.

Unlike conventional management practices, the DDP approach begins with recognizing uncertain and unpredictable outcomes. Consequently, you must discover new ideas and deliberately pivot or redirect resource allocation as reality unfolds. DDP is the foundational principle for the *capital optimization* approach essential in the idea-to-thriving part of the journey—invest small amounts of money to get specific outcomes and data you need to invest more informed in the following steps. Link your planning to small chunks of capital you can afford to lose to gain better insights to move forward. Link your progress on the CRL scale to chunks of capital rather than timeline points.

The RFF statements may still be published conventionally, with revenue at the top and profit at the bottom of the statement. You must *stand upside down* to review the bottom line first against targets for the month and validate the assumptions on indirect (discretionary) costs and direct costs up to the revenue achievement. For most ventures, especially the DeepTech ventures, revenues may not show up for several months. Therefore, the leading indicators towards revenue are essential to review.

Many founders get casual when it comes to revenue projections. First, you must make your revenue projections only based on unit sale projections. Units of sale are easier to estimate and track against actuals rather than revenue numbers. Derive your revenue stream projections only based on the volume of units you expect to sell and service, based on the firm's capacity, in an accessible market, also known as the *Serviceable Obtainable Market (SOM.)*

WHAT IS THE QUALITY OF YOUR EARNINGS?

As you build the quality of your product, process and customer experience, it is important to pay attention to the *quality of revenue* and *quality of earnings*. The policy adopted by the firm regarding what is included in reporting revenue and calculating operating profits or EBITDA indicates these qualities. For instance, one time money received by selling an asset or serving an opportunistic market need (e.g., a consulting project in a product company) must be excluded from calculating EBITDA and recognize it as "other income" after computing EBITDA. Similarly, capitalizing product development expenses that did not really resulting in creating long-term assets. In other words, the main parts of the financial reporting must be consistent with the defined business model that you intent to scaleup and grow results. It is important for founders to understand the concept of revenue and earnings quality and report only the true representation of their business model.

GOVERNANCE, RISK, AND COMPLIANCE

Governance, risk, and compliance (GRC) is a set of processes and procedures to help organizations achieve business objectives, address uncertainty, and act with integrity (8). There are three main components of GRC:

- Governance — Aligning processes and actions with the organization's business goals
- Risk — Identifying and addressing all the organization's risks
- Compliance — ensuring all activities meet legal and regulatory requirements (being a good corporate citizen.)

In the context of startups, GRC assumes great importance in avoiding significant disruption to the business that can be fatal. With a low volume of transactions and limited resources, startup firms must handle governance concerns by forming an active Board of Advisors (or expert consultants, mentors) who can act as an extension of the company's legal Board of Directors.

Risk management is the most crucial function the CEO must lead for an early-stage firm. Please see the next section for a detailed risk and crisis management discussion.

Compliance is best handled in the early years of a firm by outsourcing all the accounting and compliance processes to a competent single firm offering *virtual CFO* services.

Drivers of change can be discovered by respective signals that are relevant to the value chain, customer, and industry (e.g., industry 4.0,) trends in business models (e.g., servitization,) technological revolutions (e.g., quantum computing), etc.

IDEAS ARE EASY; EXECUTION IS EVERYTHING (9)

Creating a solid data and analytics infrastructure and culture in your firm is the only way to ensure against the lack of clarity as your firm grows. Augmenting your intuition with facts and measurements is the only way to avoid pitfalls as you make baby steps forward. You must love the process and effort of building your firm and treat the outcomes as a number on the scorecard.

Data excellence is about creating economic value using the firm's data. For an early-stage firm, it is about evidence-based scaling of the firm and using imagination to discover and build the data assets. It is also about learning using the evidence, and automating decision making for building agility for customer experience. As the firm scales up, new opportunities to monetize data would emerge. Beware of the regulations regarding data ownership and expectations to safeguard privacy and secrecy.

Be willing to adapt your worldview based on the environment as you sense and the evidence you see. It is good to have a fear of going out of business every day but want to be in business forever. Your firm's scalability and success depend on your willingness and ability to grow yourself and your team *ahead of the challenges* of scale and growth.

KEY TAKEAWAYS AND ACTION PLANNING

1. Strategy is creating a sustainable competitive advantage and growing your firm's results.
2. In the early days of your firm, most of the firm will be in discovery mode. It would be best to put a simple, practical, and dynamic measurement system in place.
3. Objectives and Key Results are critical thinking frameworks and disciplines to establish as the team starts to scale. OKRs are feasible before business processes are developed, mature, and become predictable.
4. Develop your system thinking capability to visualize the firm as a system.
5. Develop the discipline to perform a financial review of your firm using the RFF process at least once every month. Cash flow statement is the most critical statement to watch for early-stage firms.
6. Discovery-driven planning helps develop profitability targets and drive your firm toward viability and sustainability.
7. Establishing sound Governance, Risk, and Compliance management lays the foundation for a scalable firm.

CALL TO ACTION

1. Establish metrics to measure customer experience and success from the day one.
2. Establish OKRs to manage your firm.
3. Establish an RFF process with principles of Reverse Income Statement.
4. Establish processes and KPIs where possible and automate. Source external software systems to automate non-differentiating processes (e.g., expense management, CRM

etc.) and build productivity wherever feasible.
5. Establish product metrics that help monitor the product and its usage, adoption.
6. Think about and develop your data excellence strategy.
7. From a board of advisors with appropriate diversity and operational experience to support you as the founder and the board of directors.

REFERENCES

1. Richard Rumelt, "Good Strategy/Bad Strategy: The difference and why it matters," Profile Books, 2011, Kindle Edition. This is an excellent reference for founders who want to develop clarity about strategic thinking.
2. Frank, A.G.; Mendes, G.H.S.; Ayala, N.F.; Ghezzi, A. (2019). Servitization and Industry 4.0 convergence in the digital transformation of product firms: a business model innovation perspective. Technological Forecasting and Social Change, in press. https://doi.org/10.1016/j.techfore.2019.01.014 Last accessed 01-Oct-2022.
3. Ben Lamorte, "The OKRs Field Book: A Step-by-Step Guide for Objectives and Key Results Coaches," Wiley, 2022, Amazon Kindle Edition, p. 10. This book is an excellent reference for deploying the OKRs best practices in your firm.
4. Joshua Seiden, "Outcomes over Output: Why customer behavior is the key metric for business success," Sense & Respond Press, Amazon Kindle Edition, 2019, ISBN 1091173265.
5. Rita Gunther and Ian C. MacMillan, "Discovery-Driven Planning," Harvard Business Review, July-August 1995.
6. Amy Gallo, "A Refresher on Discovery-Driven Planning," Harvard Business Review Article, Feb 13, 2017.
7. Rita Gunther and Ian C. MacMillan, "Discovery-Driven Growth: A Breakthrough Process to Reduce Risk and Seize Opportunity," Harvard Business Review Press, 2009, ISBN 978-1-591-39685-7.
8. GRC (Governance, Risk, and Compliance): The Definitive Guide, https://riskonnect.com/resources/grc-guide; last

accessed 01-Sep-2022. This guide provides an excellent framework to assess the GRC maturity of firms.
9. John Doerr, "Measure What Matters," Portfolio Penguin, 2017, ISBN 978-0-241-34848-2, pp. 6.

8

MANAGE FOR RESULTS

"Dream transforms into thoughts, and thoughts result into Action."

– *Dr. A.P.J. Abdul Kalam,*

Scientist and President of India.

MARY HAD A CHATTI'S BRAIN

After many years, Dr. Mary called me again. Years ago, she met me like this when she was looking for a job after selling her firm. After that, she met me to tell me that an investor had offered to support her with seed money for a new venture. She decided to take it up as she was passionate about building her new idea—a chip based on her learning about engineering robots. It sounded like she was creating the *robot's brain*—a programmable system-on-chip that could be used for creating different kinds of robots with different capabilities. Like humans, different robots will have similar *hardware brain* but can be *trained differently* to perform different tasks! I tried to caution her. She was getting into another risky, arduous path that many founders dread. She calmly smiled, *"this time, it is different."* Entrepreneurs are crazy optimistic, aren't they? She will reach out to me whenever she needs some coaching. The last I knew was that she was making good progress with a European MNC as the first customer.

Now, Dr. Mary called and wanted to break the news privately to me that an American MNC has decided to acquire her firm. Again! She must be looking for a job. But she had a gift-wrapped box for me. I was eager to listen to Dr. Mary. And she stayed with a calm face and inquired about my family and me. The coffee arrived, and she started to sip. *"Are you looking for a job now?"* I couldn't hold my anxiety. *"No, I will be joining the MNC as VP of Engineering. They will take Chatti's Brain to the global market. Our lead customer, the European Robot maker, has committed to taking our entire production for two years!"* I couldn't get the situation. *"Why couldn't you supply to them directly?"* Dr. Mary had no confusion. *"Look, we have created the technology and product design that the Europeans loved, and a few others are in the pipeline. It is best for this American MNC to own Chatti's Brain. They have the wherewithal to proliferate this technology globally rapidly. I am happy to join them to continue the journey of Chatti's Brain. "American MNC was a strategic investor in our firm, and we know each other well. It is a great moment for us. Our team is excited!"* I sensed Dr. Mary has grown up beyond me. What is more gratifying for a coach? Am I feeling water drops in my eyes?

NATURE OF DEEPTECH VENTURES

DeepTech ventures are developing cutting-edge technology capabilities and solutions with substantial technology development efforts in computing, electronics, and physical or materials sciences. DeepTech ventures are characterized by substantial research and technology development efforts that lead to intellectual property assets in the venture. These ventures have a higher level of *uniqueness* in their solution. Certain ventures start as DigitalTech ventures and develop valuable technology assets to move their firms toward a monopolistic position.

Capturing economic value is more important than creating value. Peter Thiel (1) presents the argument for a *monopoly* business so good at what it does that no other firm can offer a close substitute. If your product is impactful, it will require less effort in distribution. Businesses that achieve that position manage to capture more economic value as sustainable profits. DeepTech firms, when successful, could become monopolies or near monopolies in their chosen niche.

Building deep technologies is about building new capabilities that improve lives. Therefore, deep technology-based solutions must address a big need with relatively low market risk. The challenge of the business is to build the technology assets that are monetized later, and therefore the need for capital. DeepTech businesses are more about the product and are characterized by market pull and sustainable profitability arising from the uniqueness.

CROSSING THREE CHASMS

Let us understand the chasms in the journey of the idea toward the firm's thriving state, as per the Triple Chasm Model (2). Please refer to the figure from Chapter 4 on Commercial Readiness Levels. In particular, it shows the presence of three transitions:

- from CRL value of 3 to 4 at **Chasm I**, which corresponds to the creation of the prototype
- from CRL value of 6 to 7 at **Chasm II**, which corresponds to the creation of the first commercially viable product
- from CRL value of 9 to 10 at **Chasm III**, which corresponds to the clarity regarding channels to market

When the firm crosses Chasm I, the focus is on technology and product development as we make customer discovery, pivots, and refine the value proposition in the context of the competition. The idea may emanate from a research lab as a technology transfer (*"lab2market"*), or a small team, including the founder, develops the prototype after sufficient customer discovery. The funding requirement at this stage must be managed to be the minimum. The only external funding sources to support crossing the Chasm I are your own or grants from incubators, governments, foundations, and corporates. The firm must file *provisional patents* for a few innovations at this stage, especially those solving a confirmed customer problem or determining an appropriate *intellectual property (IP) strategy*, which includes maintaining *trade secrets*. At this stage, the firm is resolving firm's *technology risk*, answering the question, *"Can we build it?"* DeepTech companies build assets in the early stages, which are mostly intellectual property assets.

CROSSING THE HARDEST CHASM

Research shows that crossing the Chasm-II is the hardest part of the commercialization journey (3). This chasm focuses on the *market risk*, answering the question, *"Will people buy it?"* During this period, the firm must understand the *market space* into which this product will be deployed. And *frame our value proposition precisely, in the user's and customer's language, in the competitive and regulatory environment.* The firm must strategically choose a *niche* or focus domain on targeting the solution—specific problem, application area, customer profile, geography, the form factor of the product, features of the service, and so on.

Make it as narrow as possible, watching for *unit economics (highest possible contribution margin)* and *market size*. Estimate market size starting from the unit economics definition of the unit, the volume of units the firm can deliver in a year (*Serviceable Obtainable Market or SOM*), *Serviceable Addressable Market or SAM,* and *Total Addressable Market or TAM.* Technology development and IP management continue to be necessary. This part of the journey would call for regulatory certifications too. And you must file provisional patent applications or utility patent applications for the inventions during this phase. You learn from interactions with customers and certification bodies. You continue to evolve the business model. The business model may undergo five or six iterations as the firm crosses Chasm-II. This phase's activity level and hardship are very high, as the founders must handle most of the work with a thin team and resources.

It is hard to secure venture capital funding during this phase as the market risk still needs to be fully abated. *Investment bankers (IBs)* represent investment opportunities to investors and help the firms secure investment. Most IBs will not be willing to support firms at this stage due to the low probability of success and the relatively lower transaction income of the IB. Most venture capitalists (VCs) are comfortable investing only after the firm crosses Chasm-II. As a result, many founders waste a lot of scarce time and effort chasing VCs without success. Remember, most VCs will not say "no" but engage in dialog with the founders, giving them a sense of hope.

The source of external funding at this phase would be from government and private grant schemes, accelerators, angel investors, or corporate venture capital firms. Founders must carefully evaluate and choose the appropriate investor at this phase if they are looking for external funding. We call the investors who invest at this stage *strategic investors*, as they must genuinely partner with the firm in helping it cross the Chasm-II.

Strategic investors are critical to the success of your firm. In the case of DeepTech and DigitalTech firms, it is wise to get strategic investors even if you could fund the firm's activities for scaling up. The alternative is to get credible advisors, mentors, and expert consultants who can bring substantial knowledge from operational experience. Let us collectively term them as *Strategic Partners*. Strategic partners, usually corporate VC arms, can help validate the technology implementation, support regulatory certifications, help as a go-to-market partner, introduce next-level investors, etc. You must choose Angel investors who understand the product-market space and/or deeply understand the nature of the DeepTech business from their operational experience. The strategic investments must also be timed well as you progress through the CRL levels. Choosing the strategic investors well can mean life or death for your venture.

The flip side of strategic investors can be that their weight could stifle a startup firm. Their support should not turn into interventions or interference, dictating terms to the small firm and ultimately may end up stifling innovation. Taking investment from a Customer is not a good idea. Investors could be buyers of your firm in the future but not buyers of your product/solution. Such partnerships can create several complex and conflicted situations.

THE SMALL BIG HURDLE

In comparison to Chasm-II, Chasm-III appears to be simpler for many reasons. First, if you have survived this long as a founder, you would have evolved quite a bit. Possibly, the firm has received its early venture funding, and customer revenues have started to flow. Further, the primary challenge here is to cover the *execution risk*, which answers the question, *"Can we scale up the firm?"* Your success will now depend on your firm's preparedness so far, the clarity of *strategic objectives*, prioritizing the critical activities to generate outcomes, the *technical debt*, optimally expanding the team, and starting to establish systems/processes. During this phase, the business model evolves relatively stable, with the most relevant hypotheses evidenced by facts and data. By no means is this phase easy, but you, as a founder, will likely be energized during this period as you start seeing the first pinnacle, the basecamp, a little ahead of you.

SHOULD YOU SELL YOUR FIRM?

The term *exit* in the context of startup evolution is critical to comprehend. An *exit* is when a founder or investor leaves a startup fully or partially. First, this is the opportunity to cash the shareholding in the firm with assets built in the firm and second, create an opportunity for the firm to scale further that is beyond the capabilities of the firm and its current promoters. The essential principle to understand is that exit is related to the company's value for an investor (who buys the firm partially) or an acquirer (who buys the firm fully.) When the firm grows and executes with good fundamentals, it will be valued highly by investors or acquirers. As in the case of Dr. Mary in the story above, the founder can decide to exit the control of the firm in the interest of the firm itself. Such acquisitions are possible after Chasm-II. Specifically for DeepTech companies that require manufacturing and global marketing capabilities, it is a practical way to scale the solution for the vast proliferation of the technology.

Can a firm be built to sell versus grow towards a thriving state and list in the public stock markets? In practical terms, there is very little difference between the two alternatives. The firm has to progress through the CRL levels, cross Chasm-II and then strategically decide whether to sell part of the firm (raise investment) or fully (merge with a more prominent firm to scale the capabilities required to grow the firm rapidly.)

In many cases, firms fail to scale up and get acquired for a low value attributable to some assets of the firm the buyer is interested in. Often such actions will help the external investors, and hopefully, the founder, to recover a part of their investments. If the firm has significant liabilities or debts, and only the employed talent is of value to an acquiring firm, they would structure it as an "acquihire" transaction—just hiring the employees without taking on the liabilities and commitments of the firm. These are not happy endings for the firm, but they are better than a total crash landing.

IT TAKES STRATEGIC MANAGEMENT TO EXECUTE

In a competitive economy, the managers' quality and performance determine a firm's success and survival (4). We know it as *execution* or getting things done. Larry Bossidy and Ram Charan define the seven essential behaviors for execution as follows (5):

1. Know yourself
2. Know your people and know your business

3. Identify clear goals and priorities
4. Insist on realism ("Illuminate your firm")
5. Follow-through
6. Reward the doers
7. Expand people's capabilities

Accountability and delegation are concepts that go hand in hand. The accountable person may not even know how to create the deliverables but will receive the consequences of the results from those deliverables. She will rely on a *responsible* expert to deliver the deliverables.

RISK AND CRISIS MANAGEMENT ARE DIFFERENT

Every entrepreneur must internalize the difference between risk and crisis management and be prepared to deal with both. Risk management is proactive, whereas crisis management is about responding to an adverse situation. Risk management involves identifying potential risks in advance, analyzing them, and planning steps to avoid and respond to the danger if and when it materializes. On the other hand, crisis management is how an organization responds to an unexpected disruptive event that threatens to harm the organization, clients, or its stakeholders. The unfortunate disaster of the Titanic during its maiden voyage is well-known. With a proper risk and crisis management plan, the outcome of the Titanic would have been much better. This is an inspirational case study for all entrepreneurs (6).

Often inexperienced entrepreneurs put growth and profits ahead of risk analysis or barely satisfy the requirements stipulated by law. Highly successful entrepreneurs are *risk-averse*—they only take *calculated risks*. Learning how to *calculate risk* is an important capability every entrepreneur must develop.

When a threat strikes, the human tendency is to react—fight, flee, or freeze—the *3f reactions* (7). It takes prior training and conditioning of the mind to develop a considered response to the situation. Firefighters are trained to respond to a complex fire situation rather than react. Ordinary people are put through fire drills to prepare them to respond as well as possible in a fire accident situation. Similar preparation is essential for entrepreneurs to avoid being reactive in an adverse situation. Every crisis, by definition, is unanticipated. But you can prepare for it and execute your plan for maximum benefit. In the case of the Titanic, the number of lifeboat seats available was only 1,200 for 2,200 passengers (55 %.) While this indicates poor risk planning, only 705 survivors indicate poor execution of the existing plan (32%).

Rather than anticipating a crisis, an entrepreneur could anticipate the consequences of the crisis and plan a reasonable strategy—what you should and should not do. Consequences of crisis are risks with high impact and low probability of occurrence. For instance, high impact environmental event or customer attrition causing significant revenue drop, loss of a critical team member, and so on as a consequence of crisis events. The COVID-19 pandemic caused significant business losses for several businesses. Those businesses with cash reserves could handle the situation better than those without. Maintaining a healthy level of cash reserve is a reasonable crisis management plan. However, it may not be practical for most startups, especially DeepTech startups before product-market-fit.

A promising technique for such situations is *brain-swarming*—a method for innovation that helps remove the functional fixedness bias while applying resources (8). Several more passengers could have been saved in the Titanic disaster situation if the crisis management team had used the huge iceberg that hit them as an island to stand on. They could then ferry the passengers to the iceberg. There was precedence for such a rescue operation about sixty years before the Titanic disaster. Further, most accounts of the disaster report that it took more than two hours for the ship to sink. Time was another resource available to the team to develop innovative ideas to save more lives—e.g., converting dinner tables to support floatation. When meeting with death face to face, as would have happened to the crew and passengers of the Titanic, it is hard to think innovatively, you would say. That is right, and that is the reaction—freeze or flee. However, a person trained in crisis management can respond better. Possibly the survivors would be maximized close to the number of lifeboat seats provisioned—about 50%. Or, even better, closer to 100%.

The situation is no different for the entrepreneur who faces a crisis that presents the startup's death. Without preparation, the crisis would kill the enterprise, most probably. That explains why 95% of first-time entrepreneurs fail to build a lasting business and the improved odds when that entrepreneur attempts their next startup.

HOW DOES IT ALL FIT TOGETHER?

Value proposition concerns the Customer and Market. Is there a *market desire* for our product? We establish evidence of this by working on the four blocks of the business model canvas first and establishing PSF followed by PMF:

1. Value Proposition
2. Customer Segments
3. Customer Relationships
4. Channels

Now the question is: *Can we make it and deliver it consistently and at the volume the market will ask for?* We deliver the value proposition as a prototype or minimum viable product, then the minimum saleable and deployable products. We focus on building quality and repeatability (predictability) in the delivery. This establishes the Founder-Market Fit (FMF) first and the new FMF—the *Firm-Market Fit*. We establish evidence of this by working on three blocks of the business model canvas:

1. Key Activities
2. Key Resources
3. Key Partnerships

The third and crucial question is: *Is it all viable, repeatable and sustainable?* Through the Rolling Forward Forecast (RFF), we establish evidence, working on two blocks of the business model canvas:

1. Revenue Streams
2. Cost Structure

Remember that we fill all the nine blocks of the canvas with our assumptions articulated as hypotheses and work towards gathering evidence systematically in all the blocks. We work on all the blocks concurrently, and our focus shifts between blocks as we execute. Value proposition concerns the customer, and business model concerns the firm. And the firm operates these blocks in a dynamic business environment. Watch for the weather, manage yourself to survive, and benefit from its variations.

During the journey between PMF and the thriving state is the region of *business model fit (BMF.)* At BMF, *the firm has established evidence for its capability to deliver its value proposition with an optimal profit, and it can grow sustainably further.* On the CRL scale, the firm arrives at CRL10. Remember, BMF is internal to the firm and establishes evidence of your value proposition being delivered with viability, sustainability, and scalability.

Business models are dynamic, and they must evolve and change with time. As the firm succeeds with mainstream customers, it will start experiencing the intensity of direct competition. The journey towards the firm's maturity begins now, which is about *market innovations.* Continuously monitor your value proposition's market adoption using tools such as Net Promoter Score (NPS) or Earned Growth Rate (EGR) (9) and establish agile business systems in the firm to respond.

ON FAILURES AND LUCK

Your firm's success is not about what you know or how intelligent you are. It is about how you behave, your relationship with risk, and your conviction and patience to stay at it. Anecdotal evidence indicates that it takes about seven years or more for an idea to grow beyond BMF. You have heard enough about successful leaders not giving up on failures or setbacks. *John C. Maxwell's "Failing Forward"* is an excellent reference for dealing with failures (10). Learning from setbacks will eventually get you success. But being right is often the enemy of staying right. Hugely successful leaders handled their success well and aimed higher. All successful founders also are associated with stories of luck or serendipity. Is there a science-based pattern or framework, or process to create serendipity? Dr. Christian Busch provides practical guidelines for improving your luck (11).

If you are ready with the blueprint and the evidence for a scalable firm, that addresses a large and lucrative market opportunity, you are ready to engage with investors. But wait, how will you establish that you could succeed in realizing this vision? Building lasting enterprises is about building institutions, and it is indeed a team sport. People are at the cornerstone of your strategy, and it starts with you, the founder.

KEY TAKEAWAYS AND ACTION PLANNING

1. Developing customer-centricity is essential for the firm to enhance the likelihood of its success.
2. DeepTech ventures may take longer to acquire customers as they build the assets first. Therefore, the customer acquisition rate must be higher than firms acquiring customers sooner.
3. Early investors must be chosen strategically as partners in building the firm.
4. For DeepTech firms, merging with a more prominent firm

may be the appropriate strategy to proliferate innovation widely and rapidly. In such cases, allocating a larger share of capital for building valuable assets and protecting intellectual property is more appropriate than growing the customer base.

5. Don't underestimate the need to develop your management skills.
6. Risk and crisis are different, as are the approaches to managing them.
7. Develop the strategy for scale and plan the key activities, resources, and partnerships.
8. Monitoring and balancing the revenue streams and cost structures is an essential element of building viability and sustainability.
9. If you have the evidence for building a rapidly scalable and repeatable process that can generate high quality earnings, you are ready to engage with potential investors.

CALL TO ACTION

1. Develop an appropriate intellectual property management strategy for the firm early—not filing patents due to omission or lack of capital could significantly impact the firm's value.
2. Use Value Proposition Canvas, Market Opportunity Navigator, and Business Model Canvas to design and manage the firm's business model towards BMF and beyond.
3. Develop an appropriate *exit strategy* early in the firm's life based on the nature of the idea and the business model.
4. Monitoring and managing risks is essential to the firm. Create a system for risk management early.
5. If appropriate, develop a crisis management strategy and plan "drills" to prepare the team to develop resilience.
6. Establish a Net Promoter Score-based customer listening

process to listen to the *customer's experience* as you launch your prototype or minimum viable product and make it part of your firm's DNA. Building the Earned Growth Rate (EGR) is the new and improved way to monitor the successful adoption of the innovation.

REFERENCES

1. Peter Thiel, Blake Masters, "Zero to One: Notes on Start Ups, or How to Build the Future, 2014, Random House; 2014th edition, ISBN 978-0-75355-519-4, pp.24-25.
2. Uday Phadke, Shailendra Vyakarnam, "Camels, Tigers & Unicorns," World Scientific, 2018, ISBN 978-1-786-34322-2, pp. 50-52.
3. Uday Phadke, Shailendra Vyakarnam, "Camels, Tigers & Unicorns," World Scientific, 2018, ISBN 978-1-786-34322-2, pp. 51.
4. Peter F. Drucker, "The Practice of Management," Harper Collins, 1986, ISBN 978-0-060-87897-9, pp.3. This book was first published in 1954. It is the first book to talk about Objectives and Key Result Areas.
5. Larry Bossidy and Ram Charan, "Execution: The Discipline of Getting Things Done," Random House Group, 2011, ISBN 978-1-847-94068-1, pp. xxii-xxxi.
6. Amanda M. Hicks, https://www.polleyinsurance.com/blog-1/the-titanic-before-during-after-a-case-study-in-risk-amp-crisis-management (last accessed: 25-Jun-2022.)
7. Source: https://en.wikipedia.org/wiki/Fight-or-flight_response (last accessed: 25-Jun-2022)
8. Tony McCaffrey and Jim Pearson, "Find Innovation Where You Least Expect It," Harvard Business Review, 2015.
9. Fred Reichheld, "Winning on Purpose," The Unbeatable Strategy of Loving Customers," Harvard Business Review Press, 2021, ISBN 978-1-647-82178-4. Next level of evolution of NPS and the right way of using NPS in your firm to conduct experiments and ensure continuously improving customer experience. Refer to the companion website URL: https://www.netpromotersystem.com for more information.
10. John C. Maxwell, "Failing Forward: Turning Mistakes into

Steppingstones for Success," Maxwell Motivation Inc., 2000, ISBN 13-978-0-7852-7430-8.
11. Dr. Christian Busch, "Connect the Dots: The Art and Science of Creating Good Luck," 2022, Penguin Life, ISBN 978-0241402122: This book gives several actionable ideas to pick from for creating your serendipity.

9

GROW YOURSELF AND YOUR TEAM

"Which is more important," asked Big Panda, "The journey or the destination?"

"The company," said Tiny Dragon.

— James Norbury, Big Panda and Tiny Dragon. (1)

COMING TOGETHER TO START

Naren and John were peers at the firm they had worked together. It was Naren's last day at work, and many met him and wished success for his startup. John showed up and said, *"I am joining you."* Naren did not have to think much. *"That is great, buddy. But I am yet to figure out what I will do."* John did not have to think much too. *"Whatever you do, I will be there to support you."* Nadia was the DeepTech architect in their team. She is a genius system designer focused on building their technology and product. She had very little to do with anything else in their firm. Progressively, Naren and John discovered they had a lot of overlap in what they were doing or trying to do.

John was responsible for sales. Naren felt he also must sell, as he is the one who really has the product idea. Nadia supported them by impressing the customers with her depth in technology and solutions, but something was missing. After a few missteps, they divided their roles. Naren to take business development roles, positioning the firm in the market, and interfacing with investors as the CEO. John to focus on decisions regarding the product, pricing, marketing, and distribution. Things still didn't improve for the firm, and John stayed on only for the personal connection. This star sales guy didn't like his scorecard. The early customer engagements weren't going well, and they were acutely short of the team to deliver. They blamed the younger generation for not being as hardworking, proactive and innovative. Naren decided to approach an advisor to help resolve the situation. Naren and John were chasing customers and investors, and there was no one doing the operational management of the team. John was clear, *"Don't expect me to do back office and how to create systems and processes."* Nadia said, *"I never managed any team. I don't like to sit and teach stupid engineers."* The three's determination to make the firm successful kept it limping along. They are missing a leader for operations. They were also missing the relationship with the industry to act as a bridge to other influencers who could help them with critical information and resources. The team was high on trust but low on candid conversations and teamwork. The advisor started to coach them and helped them discover themselves and others. Their transformation began to become the institution builders that they could be.

DEVELOP A BUILDER'S MINDSET

An innovation or idea cannot blossom until someone creates a business model around it and turn it into a product or service someone can buy. An innovator is, first and foremost, a creator—a problem-solver with a deep passion for improving something. Innovators are thinkers. A *builder* is different from an innovator. A builder creates economic energy where none previously existed.

Building is a high-degree-of-difficulty task, but natural builders want this impossible assignment (2). Edison is an excellent case of an inventor, innovator, businessman, and builder. Most people recall Edison as an inventor, not as the founder of the legendary firm General Electric (GE), US. Builders are good at starting with a spark of innovation, getting themselves surrounded by others who fan the fire, and managing them to control the fire from turning wild.

It is a good practice that the builder, the primary founder/CEO, owns more than half of the startup equity of the firm. It is highly risky for the firm to have "equal split" in the startup share among the primary founder/CEO and other co-founders. On the other hand, solo entrepreneurship is also likely to limit the scalability of the firm. The configuration of the startup ownership requires careful consideration, and informed decision-making.

SCALING UP SELF

The first step in building the startup is committing to scaling yourself up. It means developing a deep self-understanding and committing to improving continuously. We all wonder why it does take so long to break a bad habit or learn a new way. Timothy Gallwey, in his seminal work on coaching, says, *"The player of the inner game comes to value the art of relaxed concentration above all other skills; he discovers a true basis for self-confidence, and he learns that the secret to winning any game lies in not trying too hard. (3)"*

Our journey to competence begins with *unconscious incompetence* ("I don't know what I don't know.") Then we progress to *conscious incompetence* ("I don't know this. Or, I must unlearn my ways and learn new methods.") Then we move to the *conscious competence* phase—we apply our new learning but clumsily. Do you remember the early days you learned to ride a bicycle, shaking thoroughly and falling occasionally? You must persist through this phase to graduate to *unconscious competence* or *relaxed concentration,* as Timothy Gallewey calls it. When we reach this state, we often forget the pains of falling and hurting.

While a lot has been written about management, the day-to-day life of the founder is very challenging, with difficult questions and situations that the founder must resolve. Moral and ethical dilemmas (4) test the values and resolve of the founders. There are no easy answers, and getting those right most of the time is essential for the founder's success. Alisa Cohn (5), Ben Horowitz (6), and Bishan Sahai (7) are thought-provoking readings for the personal growth of the founder. Add them to your library if you maintain one.

IT TAKES COURAGE TO LEAD

Much has been written about leadership, and several leadership qualities have been brought out eloquently. All of these are relevant in different contexts. The essential leadership quality is *courage*, especially in the context of being an institution builder. Courage is fueled by conviction, and it demands sacrifice. Courage is the foundation behind many essential qualities that founders must have— humility, accountability, , critical thinking, strategic thinking, trusting others, risk-taking, open-mindedness, listening, impactful communication, determination, and so on.

When your courage oozes out, you cease to lead. A self-aware founder would sense this and work with a coach/mentor to restore the courage. Leadership development is about developing new perspectives. The following figure captures the imperatives of the founder/CEO.

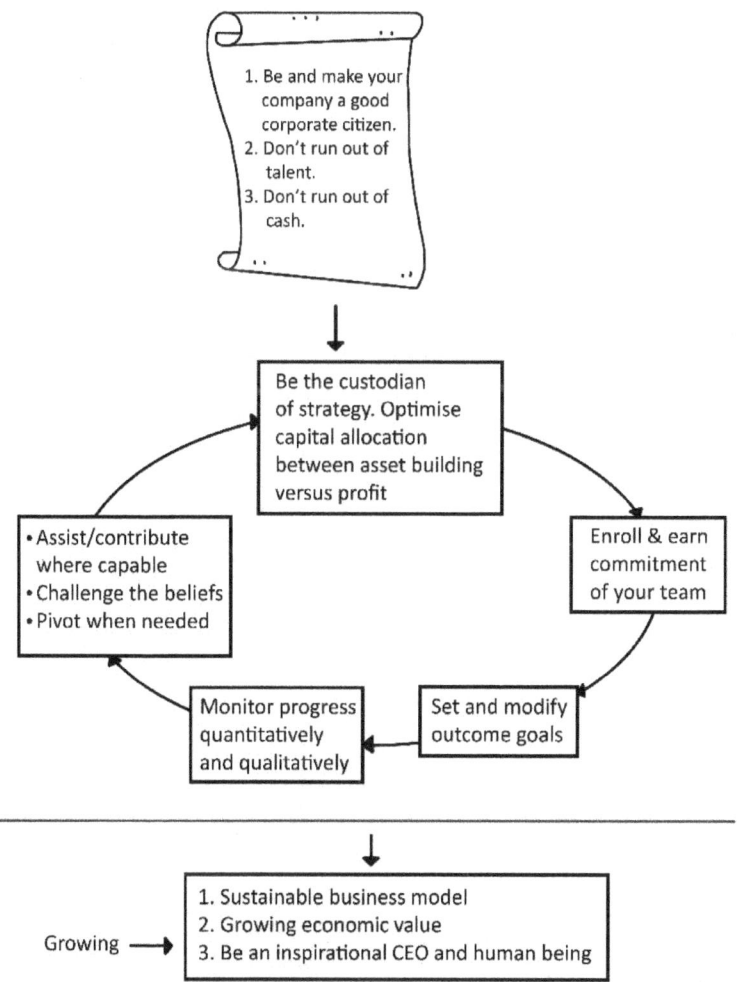

By team, it does not mean that all are full-time employees of the firm. Startups need the best of talent to help and contribute. However, the firm is not ready to afford the talent. Therefore, founders must partner for *talent on demand* or a *personal board of directors* with expert consultant, mentor, coach, advisor, investor, accountability partner, value chain partner etc.

SCALING UP THE TEAM WITH TEAMING

When we say, "*I love my job*" or "*I love what I do*," it has very little to do with the content of our work. It has everything to do with the *people we work with*. The first job of the founder builder is to build an environment where people thrive joyfully. We don't need to approve their work products when working with people we trust. When our colleagues *cooperate* with us, they support us in getting *our results*—they make us look good. When we *collaborate*, we produce results for our team and firm beyond what we could have imagined alone and guided by our shared goals.

Trust and *teaming* cannot be instructed or trained for. These must be observed, recognized, and developed by improving perspectives. Teaming is about cooperation, coordination, and collaboration in a dynamic setting. Startups need *teaming*, not just *teamwork*, and a structured collaboration with shared goals. The only way to develop teaming is by careful selection and nurturing through *Conversations, Feedback, and Recognition (CFR.)*

BUILDING YOUR TEAM

When you start with an idea, it is not practical or advisable to have a big team. It will be a small team, say 2-3 members, primarily involved in customer development and product development. However, all the functions of the firm must be handled by this team in order to operate the business. As the firm climbs up through the CRL levels, new team members must be inducted into the team to take different positions that the founding team played, one by one. Imagine the startup team to be like a soccer team. Every team member has their position defined. But the players run around the playground during the game to defend and score goals. In the early months, fewer players run to all positions, and progressively new members enter to take positions fulfilled by early members.

THIS BOOK IS NOT FOR EDISON

CUSTOMER

Where	When		How	Why	Monetization	
Support	Operation	Development	Technology	Product	Marketing	Sales
	Corporate Development Strategy			Business Development (Growth)		
People/Culture, Financials, Data/Information visibility (cognition)						
Integrative execution (CEO)						
Governance (Board of Directors)						

Ecosystem
Investors, Goverment, Universities, NGOs, Industry Bodies

Partners
- GTM/BIZ Partners
- Advisors
- Consultants

Partners
- Suppliers
- Service Providers
- Coach
- Mentor
- Incubator

For instance, when a startup is in CRL3, the most important functions are Business Development (BD) and Technology Development (TD.) No one else can if you can't sell your firm's value proposition. So, initially, the founder must hold BD while leading TD as well, possibly.

Expert consultants, interns and temporary workers can augment the bandwidth of the early team by taking ownership of specific areas and tasks (e.g., book-keeping & accounting, digital marketing, etc.) In the earliest days of your firm, you must start getting support from high-quality leaders and experienced managers as trainers, mentors, coaches, or advisors.

As the firm progresses, Business Development progressively spawns product management. Newcomers can fulfill marketing and sales positions only after PMF. You must assume a significant effort from your side to develop the newcomers into roles that you were performing initially and do it earlier than later. Scaling middle management is the toughest talent management challenge.

Do your functional leaders know how to architect and implement scalable systems? Have they worked in companies that grew rapidly? Can we find external mentors who can support the middle management to create scalability in the firm? One tip based on experience is to look for candidates from organizations ahead in the product evolution curve but not too far ahead. i.e., individuals who have worked their careers entirely in market-leading established incumbent firms would have been conditioned to work in a structured, systematic environment with practically no resource constraints to do their jobs. They would struggle to establish such systems and processes in a young firm with limited resources. Instead, professionals who have gone through the stage the startup is currently in and have grown through the scaling up to thriving stages will have valuable learning to bring to the startup. They would also fit easier with the culture. On the other hand successful employees of mature, marketing leader firms with systematic processes may find it hard to contribute to the scaling up phase of a startup firm when they must design and establish systems and processes.

KNOW YOUR GENERALS

The founder needs at least three strong generals to grow the firm to a thriving state successfully. When you start the startup, be prepared to perform these three functions, with some help from consultants and advisors.

- **Technology**: In a DeepTech or DigitalTech startup, there is no revenue and profits without an innovative product/service. Even though this book addresses very little about the technical aspects, it is the key function to start with. Technologist founders must find the appropriate support to take responsibility for product development and delivery, as most of founder's time will be required to support BD and raise venture capital in most cases. Mentoring a team of product developers to augment bandwidth is essential to build a startup. If you prefer confining to the technology areas, you must find a CEO whose leadership you are willing to accept and be accountable to.
- **Business Development (BD)**:— Pre-PMF, this role in a startup combines Product Management (Customer Development,) Marketing (Demand generation,) Sales (Closing the deal to secure purchases,) and Customer Success (ensuring positive customer experience) functions. Usually, the BD function is best performed by the founder CEO unless there is a co-founder who has internalized the purpose and vision of the founder. Progressively this role expands into multiple leaders as the firm builds scalability to support growth.
- **Finance**: One of the three key generals of your team to ensure the health and safety of the firm and watch out for the details the founder does not have the bandwidth for.

Initially, this role could be performed by a well-qualified, trusted advisor who may not have a whole-time role but whole-mind engagement. A full-time CFO will be necessary after the firm receives substantial investment from venture capital sources. Wise founders would identify an appropriate co-founder well ahead of raising capital to step into this role full-time as capital arrives in the bank.

GALLUP'S BUILDER TALENTS AND TYPES

Gallup's *Builder Profile 10* presents a psychological approach to venture building and provides a framework and tools to understand who they are, what energizes them, and what they naturally contribute (8) (9). This framework identifies ten talents that influence behaviors and best explain a builder's success. Every builder uses some mix of these ten talents.

Please note that the words that denote *talents* are precisely defined in Gallup's framework, and their English meaning should not be taken in this context.

- **CONFIDENCE**: You accurately know yourself and understand others.
- **DELEGATOR**: You recognize that you cannot do everything and are willing to contemplate a shift in style and control.
- **DETERMINATION**: You persevere through difficult and seemingly insurmountable obstacles.
- **DISRUPTOR**: You exhibit creativity in taking an existing idea or product and turning it into something better.
- **INDEPENDENCE**: You do whatever needs to be done to build a successful venture.
- **KNOWLEDGE**: You constantly search for information relevant to growing your business.
- **PROFITABILITY**: You make decisions based on

observed or anticipated effects on profit.
- **RELATIONSHIP**: You possess high social awareness and an ability to build relationships that are beneficial your organization's survival and growth.
- **RISK**: You instinctively know how to manage high-risk situations.
- **SELLING**: You are the best spokesperson for your business. Orthogonal to the talents, BP10 also identifies the type of alpha builder you are likely to be. BP10 defines them as follows.
- **RAINMAKER**: Primarily focused on generating revenue for the venture. Has unusual drive and persistence, rare grit, and focus on money-making. Obstacles and failure actually increase a rainmaker's determination. An enterprise virtually never works without this player.
- **CONDUCTOR**: Has great management ability. This is the operations person or manager who knows how to get all players on the team to work together seamlessly. Brings order and harmony to the chaos of a young venture. This person holds the whole organization together.
- **EXPERT**: Primarily focused on product development and research for the venture. Provides differentiating expertise to the core product or service. Every successful startup has an alpha expert who distinguishes it from the crowd. Being the best in their field matters to them most.

The Builder Profile 10 is presented here only to create awareness of such a model for founders. You must use Gallup's online assessment tool and the services of a Gallup-certified coach on BP10 to use this framework effectively.

The ideal startup management team is three individuals of each profile with some history of working together, about the same age, and financial standing with mutual respect and aligned values. Most successful firms project a "single founder" who leads an aligned team of co-founders, or entrepreneurial employees, who take situational leadership and often stay away from the limelight. The founder/CEO for the team may come with any of the alpha builder profiles.

COMPANY MATTERS MOST

Most firms collapse before achieving a thriving state because of internal problems among key leaders than due to competition or external challenges. In his book, *The Founder's Dilemma*, Harvard Business School professor Noam Wasserman quotes a survey finding that 65% of high-potential startups fail due to conflict among co-founders (10). And one of the primary reasons for conflicts is misaligned goals among the co-founders. Early in your firm's evolution, you must have a candid conversation among the co-founders to explicitly call out why they are in the startup firm and get to an alignment. Founder-Market fit depends on this *"Founders Teaming Fit"*. If you couldn't align the co-founders early, it is better to part ways early than later when the stakes are high.

If you want what people bring, you must give them what they need. Periodically, you must take the time collectively to know what you need and what others need. Find the time to spend together every day during the initial years. If not practical, every week. If anyone tries to keep the interaction minimal, it indicates mutual avoidance and the upcoming conflict. Successful founders embrace conflict—conflict doesn't destroy strong teams because they focus on results. They constantly resolve conflicts and grow. If you didn't prepare for conflict in your co-founder relationship, you would be at each other's throats right when you most need to collaborate effectively.

In the arduous startup climb, what we cherish long after will be the company of people we had and what we built together. So, choose your company carefully. And establish a trusted relationship through mutual actions. Key aspects of the relationship should be reduced to a *founder agreement* when appropriate. Getting the services of an executive coach for the founders is a best practice to support team building and resolving conflicts.

HOW TO CASTRATE A BULL?

Accountability and empowerment are the most complex and impactful elements of culture that you build in your firm. And if you can do it from day one, no one can stop your firm. And it starts with you!

In the 1960s, scientist Derek De Solla Price created a law that essentially quantifies *social loafing*. He found that *roughly the square root of the number of people in an organization contributes to 50% of the work* (11). Such ideas help model the world and consciously create differentiation. That is why your startup with fewer team members could outperform larger organizations. First, look for team members with a track record of asymmetric contributions. Social loafing is less likely in an organizational culture when one or more of the following exists. Employees feel that their work is important and meaningful. Employees can see the relationship between their work and successful outcomes. Individual employees like each other; working in this team is valuable and important to them. Leaders demonstrate that they identify, evaluate, and appropriately recognize individual contributions.

Startup team members must be able to converse with each other with respectful candor. Conflicts among early team members are normal, and they should not break the teams if everyone is focused on results. Members of strong teams are as committed to their personal lives as they are to their work. And strong teams respect and embrace diversity. A good indicator of a strong team is when it acts as a *talent magnet*. In similar lines to PMF, you will start observing the firm's employees referring top talent to the firm without any big referral bonus, and top talent applying directly to the firm will be on the increase.

Building your firm's "right culture" is a crucial reason for successfully scaling your firm. Culture is the founder's accountability—you build it by behaving and responding. The culture of firms can develop to become a competitive advantage or an inhibitor of growth. Dave Hitz, technical co-founder of NetApp has narrated an inspiring story on building a positive culture at NetApp, a bay area DeepTech company. (12).

HOW TO MANAGE INDIVIDUAL PERFORMANCE

One of the crucial aspects of scaling your team is performance assessment and talent development. The firm may not have formal systems and tools for the initial few years. However, the process must exist from day one that the founder personally owns. Only by managing the talent the right environment can be established in the firm.

The reference point for assessment is the goals of the firm and individual goals agreed mutually. In a startup team, it is not practical to work with well-defined job descriptions. But goal setting is the foundation to manage organization results, culture, and individual performance. This must start on the day the firm adds the second person.

Using an even-numbered scale to assess is more effective, even though ratings may not be done formally in the early days.

1. Below expectations or unacceptable
2. Meets expectations
3. Occasionally exceeds expectations
4. Performs at a higher level compared to most

The logic of this scale is to differentiate well-performing team members clearly. Conversations, Feedback and Recognition (CFR) is the only organization process in the early years to assess and develop talent. Two distinct processes are recommended to manage talent retention and development.

1. **Retention**: Assess the team member on two dimensions—

Results (outcomes) and Trust & Teaming. The ideal quadrant is both scores high. Individuals who are low on Trust & Teaming may not be appropriate to recognize and retain in the organization, even if they are high on Results.

2. **Development**: Assess the team members on two dimensions—Performance (effort and outcomes achieved) versus Potential to perform a higher-level role (education, experience, behavior, etc.) The ideal quadrant is both scores high, which is usually less than 10% of the population. Those with high potential but lower performance are candidates for different roles, matching their potential. Those with high on performance and lower potential are candidates for learning & development if they aspire to grow to higher levels in the firm.

OKRs and Net Promoter Score (NPS) indicate the results of the firm's effectiveness and culture. Using these measures to measure individual performance will lead to unsustainable results. Sales and service people begging customers for a higher NPS score is indeed the wrong way to use NPS. Falling short in achieving OKRs and NPS targets must trigger organizational root cause discussions and learning, not individual blaming.

All assessments are done by the founders and managers of the firm initially. Progressively, as the firm matures beyond Business Model fit and closer to the thriving state, more formal processes can be considered appropriate to the culture.

EVERYONE NEEDS A COACH

Bill Gates started his TED talk (13) (14) with the statement, "*Everyone needs a coach.*" Every successful founder has received support from effective coaches who help them uncover their blind spots, develop realistic self-awareness, and personally grow to meet the challenges of building the firm. Coaches offer observations, outside-in perspectives, objective insights, and tools to handle the executive's different situations, including conflicts with others.

KEY TAKEAWAYS AND ACTION PLANNING

1. Develop a builder's mindset.
2. Leadership development is perspective development.
3. The primary founder/CEO must own more than half of the equity in the firm.
4. Three essential CEO commandments are: Don't run out of money and talent; and don't break the law.
5. You cannot train for trust and teaming.
6. Use NPS, OKRs and CFR to empower and align your team to drive for results.
7. Do not use OKRs progress and NPS score to assess any individual's performance (other than the founder/CEO).
8. Leverage "talent on demand."
9. Strive to balance among technology, business development, and finance.
10. Strive to establish an interdependent leadership team of rainmaker, conductor, and expert (Gallup Builder Profile 10)
11. Accountability and empowerment are the most complex and impactful elements for creating the culture of a scaleable firm.
12. Goal setting and talent management are crucial management processes to establish from the day one.
13. Everyone needs a coach.

CALL TO ACTION

1. Articulate the purpose ("why"), values ("how") and vision & mission ("what") of your firm.
2. Establish goals (3-5 years), Objectives (1-2 years.) Use these to establish OKRs for the next 2-4 months.
3. If you have started delivering your product to customers, conduct a simple NPS survey to listen learn.

4. Establish a diverse advisory board to advise and mentor you and your team.
5. Establish a talent management system, however simple it is.
6. Do you have a coach to support you?

REFERENCES

1. James Norbury, Big Panda and Tiny Dragon https://www.penninn.is/en/book/big-panda-and-tiny-dragon last accessed 29-Jul-2022.
2. Jim Clifton and Sangeeta Badal, "Born to Build: How to Build a Thriving Startup, A Winning Team, New Customers and Your Best Life Imaginable," Gallup Press, 2018, ISBN 978-1-595-62127-6. This seminal work is grounded on Gallup team's years of research on entrepreneurs and institution builders. This book offers a psychological approach to venture building.
3. W. Timothy Gallwey, "The Inner Game of Tennis: The Classic Guide to the Mental Side of Peak Performance," Pan Publishing, ISBN 978-1447288503, 2015.
4. The Sanskrit term *dharma-sankat* accurately depicts these situations—there are no easy answers.
5. Alisa Cohn, "From Start-up to Grown-up: Grow Your Leadership to Grow Your Business," Kogan Page Limited, 2022, ISBN 978-1-398-60138-3.
6. Ben Horowitz, "The Hard Thing about Hard Thing: Building a Business When There Are No Easy Answers," Harper Business, 2014, ISBN 978-0-062-27320-8. Ben brings out practical difficulties in running a startup and building an enduring culture in your firm.
7. Bishan Sahai, "Dilemma: Management Book of Questions," Academic Foundation, 2021, ISBN 978-93-327-0569-2. This book does not provide any answers. It allows the reader to exercise their mind on complex situations.
8. Gallup Builder Profile 10, URL: https://www.gallup.com/builder/225332/builder-profile-10.aspx Last accessed 01-Oct-2022.
9. Jim Clifton and Sangeeta Badal, "Born to Build: How to Build a Thriving Startup, A Winning Team, New Customers and Your Best Life Imaginable," Gallup Press, 2018, ISBN

978-1-595-62127-6, pp. 26-27.
10. Noam Wasserman, "The Founders' Dilemmas: Anticipating and Avoiding the Pitfalls that Can Sink a Startup," Princeton University Press, 2021, Amazon Kindle Edition, pp. 493. Survey by Gorman and Sahlman, 1989.
11. Barry Dunaway, "Another Reason Companies Fail: Price's Law," 20-Feb-2020, URL: https://www.am1st.com/another-reason-companies-fail-prices-law: Last Accessed 01-Oct-2022.
12. Dave Hitz and Pat Walsh, "How To Castrate a Bull: Unexpected Lessons on Risk, Growth, and Success in Business," Jossey Bass, 2009, ISBN 978-0-470-34523-8.
13. https://www.youtube.com/watch?v=81Ub0SMxZQo: Bill Gates, "Teachers need real feedback" TED Talk, (2013), accessed on 20-Jan-2022.
14. https://www.youtube.com/watch?v=oHDq1PcYkT4: Atul Gawande, "Want to get great at something? Get a coach," TED Talk (2018), accessed 20-Jan-2022. This is an impactful talk that explains the role of the coach very well.

10

RAISE CAPITAL AS A PRO

"Raising venture capital is the easiest thing a startup founder is ever going to do."

– Marc Andreessen, Cofounder, and General Partner (1)

MARY HAD A LITTLE STARTUP

It was a pleasant surprise to receive a call from Dr. Mary. Last month she was in the news. An American MNC acquired her firm, and she must be rich. As if it was yesterday, I vividly remember Mary's wide-open eyes and animated pitch when she said, "All *I need now is someone who believes in me and gives me the seed capital. My problems will be over, and we will be on our way.*" Now she wanted to thank me and start discussing her next venture, as many successful founders do, I imagined. The coffee shop was empty and quiet. Mary was even more silent, occasionally smiling awkwardly as we waited for our coffee. As we sipped the coffee, I was eager to listen to Mary. "*I am sorry I wasn't in touch with you since we met last. You know how startup life is. I was too busy. Now, will you please help me find a well-paying job quickly?*" She broke her silence, and her voice was not confident. I could sense something was wrong. Indeed, she got an exit, but a *liquidation preference* had hit her. Straight out of her Ph.D. to start the firm, she had no clue what the term meant—"they" said it was a "standard clause" in the *investment agreement* with investors. She understood the clause well by now—she received 15K USD instead of 1.5 M USD from the acquisition! "The Board" believed the firm was not growing fast enough. She couldn't stop the acquisition of "her" firm as she was "outvoted" and out by the Board. She couldn't afford a lawyer to fight for her. She worked hard on a valuable idea and executed it well to make someone else richer.

YOU CAN'T TELL A GREAT STORY IF YOU DON'T HAVE ONE

Most founders say raising capital is the biggest challenge to progress with their firm. If you came to this chapter straight away without reading the rest of the book, eager to learn how to raise capital, please go back and read—at least the key takeaways at the end of each chapter—before reading further. You should go forward with this chapter only if you have decided and are ready to raise equity capital for your firm in exchange of equity shares of your ownership. If you do not want to raise equity capital for your firm anytime, you can skip this chapter and return to it when considering that option.

Many incubators and trainers have popularized the belief that raising capital is about storytelling. Techie founders undergo *scriptwriting* mentoring, *method acting* courses, and *elevator pitch* competitions (the equity-free prize money is good, though.) They believe that the best entrepreneurs are not the best visionaries. *The greatest entrepreneurs are incredible salespeople. They know how to tell an amazing story that will convince talent and investors to join the journey, says Marc Andreessen* (2). While Marc and others are right, it must be understood in the right context and perspective. Don't raise funding *like* a professional but *be* a professional. Your starting point for raising capital is to have a *fundable* business model. The purpose of storytelling is to keep the attention and engagement of the audience when you have something important to say. And realize that investing is an emotional decision supported by a reasonable rationale to justify it.

Very few founders succeed in raising capital—one-in-ten or twenty, let us say. And in each new round, investors use finer filters.

BE STRATEGIC ABOUT THE FIRST INVESTORS

It is very hard to get capital in the early stages of the firm, before CRL7. Especially in the case of DeepTech ventures, wherein revenue cannot start even within few years, your efforts must be focused on securing *non-dilutive* ("equity free") *grants* from the government and private sources. Such grants are available to support technology, product development, patenting etc. The other form of non-dilutive capital is various forms of debt; for e.g., debt against purchase orders from credible buyers, or revenues. All the forms of capital available in exchange of equity shares or convertible instruments (e.g., compulsorily convertible debentures) are termed as *venture capital* in this chapter; be it a small percentage for an incubator or angel investor.

Venture capital comes broadly in different classes of investors—individual (or angel) investors, Family Fund Offices (FFO,) Corporate Venture Capital (CVC,) Venture Capital (VC,) and Private Equity (PE) firms. Angel investing is appropriate in the very early stages of CRL3 to CRL7. *Incubators* also support startups in this stage and give access to mentors and investors. *Accelerators* are appropriate as the firm matures to CRL6. It is prudent to join an incubator or accelerator, especially for first-time entrepreneurs.

Large enterprises invest in startups based on their strategic reasons, relatively less motivated by direct financial investment returns. CVC has been consistently increasing over a decade. Q3-2021 saw the peak of CVC at 50B USD in 1,377 deals. CVC has been reducing since then to 19B USD in 1,098 deals in Q3-2022 (3). Corporates also organize Accelerators to support startups typically beyond CRL5.

The class of investors in this section invest their own money. So, individuals decide to invest in a startup and the price with their personal/corporate investment philosophy. The uncertainty and risk levels are highest at this stage. Investing at this stage most often creates a binary outcome—capital lost or returned with profits. So savvy investors tend to go wide—invest in many firms. While individual results vary drastically, the annual returns for angel investing can range from 45-75%.

For the founder, this is the *first cheque* from an external investor. This investor is often a wealthy individual or a collective of such individuals (*"syndicate"*.) who become the Earliest Investors (EI.) Partnering with an appropriate EI has far-reaching consequences; so, choose EI deliberately and strategically.

Certain EI typically celebrities, are totally passive and does not provide any support to the startup other than the financial investment. Such Eis bring a certain level of credibility for the founder. If the EI understands the risks of startups, has built successful firms, or has relevant operational experience, or relationships in the startup's domain, and willing to provide some active support to strengthen the founder are more appropriate. They could play a crucial role in getting investors in the same or subsequent rounds.

EI must be willing to work with the founder and team to support navigating the CRL climb. There are no pre-determined answers during this journey—it is a phase of experimentation and learning. EI and the founder must agree on a governance process and metrics, set associated cadence, etc. EI can help you plan out the milestones for the next round of raising money and support you in negotiating with the next set of investors who typically are more sophisticated. EI typically stays in the background and support the founder. Founders must be transparent and keep the EI informed regularly and proactively. Only then could the EI help the founder as a true partner in the journey.

Investors have investor rights. Founders must honor and manage the interests of the existing investors with the demands of the new, incoming investors in the following rounds. This can be challenging. But the founder must do everything possible for them to negotiate the interest of the existing investors.

Ideal EI knows the industry the startup is trying to enter and the associated business dynamics. Founders must take serious care in making choices and decisions at this stage, anticipating obstacles and opportunities in the future.

Many founders make the mistake, often out of ignorance or desperation, of raising capital from inappropriate EI. Such EI can jeopardize further investments by posing difficult hurdles for incoming investors who typically invest larger amounts in better valuation. Or, the EI can create hard situations for the founder to make progress.

How many prospective investors should you contact before you find the right partner? Not a few, but the order of 100+, somewhat similar to customer discovery; it is *investor discovery*. It is wise to carefully choose angel investing platforms, incubators and appropriate pitching contests that have emerged in the startup ecosystem to facilitate individual investors and founders to connect (4). You must research potential investors using these platforms and seek *strategic early investors*.

The table showing the details of current shareholders of the firm with their corresponding ownership level is termed as *capital table* or *captable*. Incoming venture capital providers prefer a simple captable with as few entries as possible, besides the founders or promoters. The incoming investors will also prefer the founder to use the capital in the business rather than providing *exit opportunities* for existing investors. Founders must internalize this and carefully manage accordingly.

STEPPING UP THE GAME TO THE NEXT LEVEL

VC and PE firms manage the money they source from many sources. There are essential differences between VC and PE approaches to investment. For our purpose, let us approximate VC and PE to be the same, but the PE firms come with larger fund sizes and invest after the thriving stage, to prepare the firm for an initial public offer (IPO) or a M&A opportunity. Typical sources of money for VC and PE funds are high-net-worth individuals and families, enterprises, large investment institutions such as superannuation funds and banks, state-owned investment funds, etc. The individuals and entities who provide the money to the venture capital firm are called *Limited Partners (LP.)* The VC firm forms a *fund* to pool the money and must return the money to the LPs with capital appreciation in about ten years or less. *General Partners (GP)* are responsible for all investment decisions and typically invest their capital in the same fund. GP manages the funds and are accountable to the LP to perform as per their promise and agreement.

Venture capital firms get paid through two revenue streams: management fees and *carried interest*. Management fees are annual payments investors pay to cover operational expenses, a small fraction of the fund size. Remember, they must convince and earn the trust of the LPs to be part of and manage the VC firm. They are raising money *perpetually* on the founder's behalf. Venture capital firms have some of the industry's most talented, most thoughtful people. First, develop a rapport and respect for them.

VCs come in many shapes, sizes, and experience levels. For instance, incubators and accelerators may be tiny VCs in disguise. Investors assess the founder (and team), business model, and business strategy. Nothing convinces the VC better than the track record of executing strategically and evidence of growth. Nathan Reiff gives a good overview of the different stages of VC funding (5).

Investors evaluate the founder and critical team members for trustworthiness and coachability, besides their functional capabilities. The personality of the lead founder or founding CEO contributes significantly to the investment decision. Handle investors with respect, even when you get a negative response to your ideas or views. You can respectfully disagree and move on.

Investment banking (IB) is a professional service that provides financial consultancy services and helps firms raise capital. They act as intermediaries between firms and investors. When the size of capital to be raised is large and the gestation period is high, startup firms must consider using the services of IB firms. IB provides professional guidance to prepare rigorously, bring investor relationships, and will charge a combination of retainer fee, share of capital raised and equity.

EMPATHIZE WITH THE INVESTOR

Many deeply technical founders need help communicating with investors. This difficulty stems from the disconnect between what the investor wants to hear and what the founder wants to tell. Empathize with the investor and help them make their decision. They would ask if you missed telling them something they wanted to hear. So, be an effective listener and "to the point" contextual communicator.

Naturally, as the founder, you will be more passionate about your product/solution and possibly your customers. Investors are more interested in whether the business will generate financial returns they expect. Investors want to know who wants your product and why, how big the market opportunity is, and how soon it can be monetized. They want to learn as much as possible about you, the founder, because their bet is ultimately on you. It is indeed a big responsibility. Individual investors and General Partners of VC firms who make the investment decision often ask, "Why did you start this startup?"

Following this, you must answer the questions to the investors: Is there a large market opportunity? Is there money to be made in this market opportunity? Why are you the right team to make money from this opportunity? How much return will the business generate for the investment in 5-7 years or sooner?

The strength of the secondary and, more importantly, the primary research (what you directly found from the customer interactions) influence the investor's decision. External conditions will also influence the investment decision (e.g., regulatory impact of the sector/business, competitive landscape, the possibility of hostile takeovers, etc.) Ultimately, why don't they invest? Here is a very informative article from an investor with several valuable tips for founders (6).

Investors want to know who is watching the money and whether their money will be handled with care. Introduce your *good CFO* and announce your plan for governance—how would you ensure good use of money? Present your operational metrics, not high-level visions. Keep a systematic record of meetings and follow through.

MIND THE FUNDRAISING CHASM

It becomes relatively easier to get venture capital after CRL10, if you have established the business model that can grow profits rapidly using capital to scaleup the firm's capacity. Typically, the firm has achieved some revenue in the vicinity of 250-500K USD and has the potential to win more income soon, as evidenced by a strong pipeline. The equity given up in exchange for seed funding is generally 10–20% for an investment of about 1-2M USD. Let's say the firm received 2M USD for 20% equity. That means the VC is pricing (valuing) the firm at 10M USD, after the investment. The seed investor VC is usually the first institutional investor in the firm, and the firm is poised for rapid growth towards the next round of investment, ideally in three years. At that time, the firm's valuation (i.e., price in the VC investment market) should have grown at least three times or 30M USD. Of course, the higher, the better.

Usually, the next investment round is called the Series-An investment, and the investment amount is, let's say, 6M USD in exchange for 20% equity of the firm. That translates to the pricing of the firm at least 30M USD. This example is a reasonably happy situation. However, if the seed funding was 2M USD for 10% of the firm, the pricing at the seed funding level is 20M USD. The seed investor will not be happy with a 25M USD valuation after three years but would expect about 60M USD valuation. This means the firm has to show evidence of progress in economic value. Therefore, there is a strategic tradeoff about how much money to raise, at what pricing (valuation,) and when. This decision is unique to the firm's evolution of business model and execution characteristics. The strategy is like designing *gravitational slingshots* to propel a spacecraft. Less than 10% of companies that raise a seed round successfully raise a Series A investment (7). This climb is steep and strenuous.

UNDERSTANDING THE CAPITAL RAISING GAME

Early investors don't value startups;
They price them! (8)

Aswath Damodaran's video class on *Valuing Young Companies* (9) is a good reference for finance professionals and founders willing to listen through an intense finance modeling class to pick up a few nuggets of wisdom.

You can value an asset based on its fundamentals (cash flows, growth, and risk) or price it based on what others pay for similar assets. The two can yield different numbers. As early-stage firms are building assets and are not predictably profitable, buyers can only price them. VCs follow *exit-based planning* or "starting with the end in mind." This process embeds much business knowledge and dynamics in approximating the firm's future results using known patterns or *buckets*. So, it is a matter of negotiation and not a consistent estimation.

Year	0	1	2	3	4	5	6	7
Target valuation	0	3	6	9	12	15	18	21
Founders	100%	80%	64%	64%	51%	51%	41%	37%
Individual Investors		20%	16%	16%	13%	13%	10%	9%
VC Round 1			20%	20%	16%	16%	13%	12%
VC Round 2					20%	20%	16%	14%
VC Round 3							20%	18%
VC Round 4								10%
Total	100%	100%	100%	100%	100%	100%	100%	100%

DEEPTECH FIRMS BUILD ASSETS FIRST

Revenue growth and rate of profit growth are the only solid indicators of the early adoption of a product and the firm's execution capability. So, most investors prefer firms with revenue achievement. Raising capital for DeepTech firms is significantly more challenging, as the uncertainty, gestation capital, and time to revenue are considerably higher. Most VCs want to see a short cycle time for investment and exit. Those VCs are appropriate for DeepTech firms only after the revenues begin. However, there are VCs whose *investment thesis or philosophy* is aligned with your firm's roadmap for long gestation or social impact firms. It would be best to discover such VC firms to work with and not waste time with most of the regular VC firms. See the reference below for an example of investors focused on Quantum Computing startups. (10)

For instance, if your firm is into manufactured components, medical devices, or other DeepTech ideas, the adoption curve would lie on the x-axis for a considerable time and hopefully climb steeply, as shown in the figure. In such cases, it is vital to develop the roadmap with clearly identified milestones (e.g., certifications, customer MoUs, etc.) that demonstrate the reduction of risk and uncertainty. Founders must strive to maximize the equity-free grants and onboard strategic investors who could actively partner to build the firm at this stage. You could also target CVCs and Family Fund Houses who may have an alignment with the kind of DeepTech firm you are building.

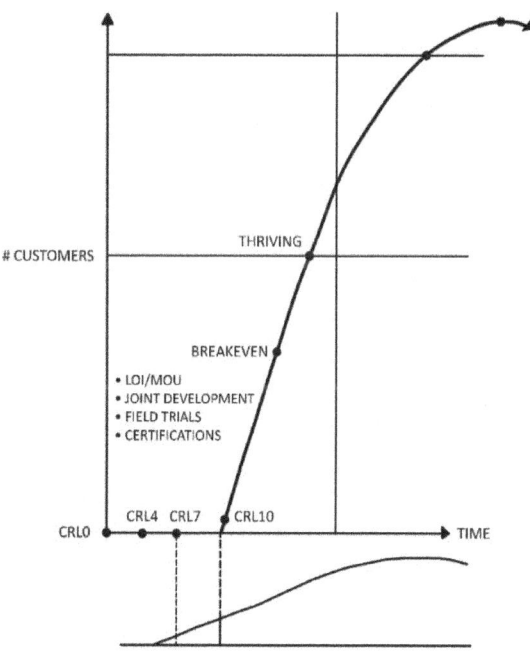

Ideally, founders must internalize and develop a sequential financing plan before venturing into such a firm. For instance, DeepTech firms that must establish a manufacturing process will take a few years before they are ready to produce their products. Such firms could consider outsourcing manufacturing to other firms to generate revenue sooner. DeepTech firms will have several inventions that can be filed as patents. Presenting the patent portfolio with its commercial value estimated by IP valuators is a way to establish asset value to investors.

MagicLeap, an augmented reality startup in the USA, raised huge funding of over 3B$ (11) capital before their product was ready. Such a level of early-stage fund-raising calls for extraordinary skills and a special investment ecosystem. It is impossible in most parts of the world or by most founders.

INVESTORS WANT TO INVEST, MAKE IT EASIER FOR THEM

We hear accounts of successful firms providing substantial financial returns to early investors. Venture-capital funds raised $151 billion in the three quarters of 2022, a year filled with anxieties about recession and geo-political challenges. This exceeds any prior full-year fundraising, according to recently released information from PitchBook Data Inc. (12) *Limited Partners* who back venture funds still seek access to startups, which have outperformed other asset classes. More individual investors are ready to invest in promising startups now than ever before. However, 2023 witnessed an "investment winter" and investment sentiment will be cyclic. The capitalistic community has an ever-increasing enthusiasm to invest in profitable ideas. Decentralization of capital is a macro trend that drives startup action.

First, start early. Very few may be lucky to close their funding in 20 working days. These founders may have over a million views for their posts in about a year, or 2000+ people network on LinkedIn. Or they have relationships established from their previous roles. You must expect a lead time of about six months or more from when you begin the pursuit to the end of receiving money in the bank. It can take longer to get a "no," making the process complex. As the investors have no incentive to say "no," they choose silence or ask you to produce some information that will take a long time.

When the firm is in its infancy (e.g., CRL8), it is tough to predict financials accurately. Savvy investors also know that. Therefore, you must demonstrate your foresight (independently verifiable assumptions) through the information you disclose. The typical process of progress with any investor is as follows.

1. Somehow, you get a gentle introduction (which is best), visit the investor's website, pitching event, or email the first level of information to the investor. This document is a short slide deck, ideally nine slides or fewer (called the *Pitch Deck*.)

This is a *self-serving* document that the investor team would review. The desired leading indicator is often a phone call and an opportunity to meet with the investor team members.

2. It typically takes 5-8 sessions before the investor gives you a term sheet (proposal to invest.) Success is getting to the next meeting each time you meet with an investor. If the firm is in its infancy, the number of sessions may be fewer, say two to three.
3. Once you get the meeting with the angel investor or the GP of the VC firm, your firm is seriously being considered for investment. Remember, good investors are free thinkers and often contrarian in their views. There is no easy way to influence them, other than being authentic and genuine. It is a mutual selection process to get funded.

ARE YOU READY TO TRAVERSE THE IDEA MAZE?

Most good investors bet on the founder (and the founding team) to make their investment decision. Be ready to discuss your idea deeper as you meet with investors. Good investor meetings would make you traverse through the *idea maze*. (13)

It does not mean that investors are technically knowledgeable about your expertise. Their approach to the discussion is comparable to an investigator questioning suspects and witnesses but in a friendly posture. Detectives do not know what actually happened, but they must get the other persons to lead them to the truth and the facts of the matter. So, they develop a style of questioning deep. As the questions get deep in the idea maze, some founders may break down, giving answers that are an apparent lie or baseless.

The only way to handle the situation is to approach it with humility. Speak the truth and do not hesitate to say, "*I don't know, but I will find out*," when that is the best answer.

How many times should you follow up with the investor after your meeting? Rarely! Every investor remembers a good investment opportunity. However, send a brief "thank you" email immediately after each session capturing actions to follow or a few (not more than 3) points or questions you took away.

Once you successfully navigate the maze, the investor gives you a *term sheet*, a non-binding document outlining the material terms and conditions of potential investment subject to a due diligence.

GET A BETTER PARTNERSHIP THAN A BETTER VALUATION

Congratulations! You have a *term sheet* now. You now have someone who likes, trusts, and believes in you to build the firm and deliver good returns for the investment. Now, the phase of *information asymmetry* begins in the partnership. Only the founder knows deeply about the firm's performance and outlook. The investor wants to protect their capital with limited visibility of the firm's performance. This information asymmetry is the root cause for the clauses in the term sheet that becomes the terms of the *shareholder agreement* later.

Agreements are written among excited friends and read in despair among adversaries. So, it is wise for the founder to take the counsel of a *good CFO* to review the term sheet together. For an overview of the term sheet, please refer to this online article (14) (15). Following are a few critical clauses in a term sheet for the founder's attention and left to you to learn about them in your context: Participating and Non-Participating, Liquidation Preference (16) (17) Anti-dilution, Pre-emptive, and pro-rata rights, ROFR and co-sale rights, voting rights, board rights, founder vesting, ESOP pool, drag-along, and tag-along rights, redemption rights, and so on. Understand their implications in your context when you are negotiating with a term sheet.

HOW MUCH TIME SHOULD A FOUNDER PLAN FOR RAISING MONEY?

Founders underestimate the time, effort, and creative energy required to get the cash in the bank, raising capital from investors. Preparation, effort, and time are the least appreciated aspect of raising money. This could have been productively applied to meeting customers, building the team, building the product, and so on, and it must be optimized. One good way to do this is to combine the time for *investor relationships* with the time the founder must allocate for the firm's financial management. This approach develops the investor mindset and associated lingo, spreading the time to reduce the peaks. After you receive the investment, you must nurture a positive relationship with your investors, who are your partners now. Establish a transparent communication channel with the investors. Understanding the investor's preferences is wise—some of them expect and even establish regular communication protocols.

The process repeats for the next round in about eighteen to thirty-six months. This combined time can be roughly 20% of the founder's time (eight hours a week.) It would be best if you managed it with discipline. Yes, the investor relationship is a substantial amount of timeshare of the founder/CEO. As your firm raises multiple investment rounds, you would require a part-time/full-time support executive to assist managing the investor relationship.

HOW TO KEEP CONTROL OF THE FIRM

Most founders, especially mission and vision-based founders, want to be in the driver's seat of "their" firm. You never want to give up your say in the firm's affairs to someone else. You must raise the minimum external capital and scale the business on *retained earnings* or re-investing profits. That way, the founder and team can remain the major shareholders. But that is not easy. Why would the investors want to change the CEO if the firm delivers exemplary corporate governance? A few imperatives of good founder/CEO behavior are: *Don't use investor's money to treat yourself with personal luxuries; be humble and be willing to change. Demonstrate integrity, transparency, and learning agility; Optimize capital utilization.*

No deal is perfect, and even the savviest founders are at a

disadvantage in negotiating with people who strike deals for a living almost daily. Founders have a strong incentive to learn as much as possible about raising money. But, the technologist founder is perhaps least interested in learning these things and wants to focus on building a world-changing product. Be willing to learn and rely on expert trusted advisors. That is why founders who build empowered, interdependent teams succeed in making legendary firms. So, raise capital as a professional, not like a professional.

KEY TAKEAWAYS

1. You must have a profitable, repeatable, scalable business model before you can narrate your story to investors.
2. Realize that investors have a different culture, language and goals, different from the technologists.
3. Choose your early investors wisely and strategically. Weak choice of early investors could hurt your firm's progress in raising sequential capital.
4. Empathize with the investors and learn the capital raising game. Make it easier for them to invest.
5. DeepTech firms must demonstrate progress in asset creation, commercial value, and protection.
6. Seek a better partnership than a better valuation in the early stages.
7. If you want to retain control of your firm, perform well growing economic value and grow trust with investors disclosing appropriately.

CALL TO ACTIONS

1. Get advice and support from a *good CFO* if you aren't doing that.
2. Create articulated market space assessment, business model, strategy, and financial model for your firm.
3. Allocate about 20% of the founder/CEO's time to review and learn the progress your firm makes in the context of

your strategy and projections (RFF.) And allocate about 20% of your time to engage with the investors, if you choose to raise external equity investment.

REFERENCES

1. Marc Andreessen, "Lecture 9: How to Raise Money," Stanford's CS183B Course How to Start a Startup, URL: https://startupclass.samaltman.com/courses/lec09: Last accessed 01-Sep-2022.
2. Alejandro Cremades, "The Art of Startup Fundraising: Pitching Investors, Negotiating the Deal, and Everything Else Entrepreneurs Need to Know," 1st Edition, 2016, Wiley, Amazon Kindle Edition, pp.14.
3. CB Insights, "State of CVC Q3'22 Report," URL: https://www.cbinsights.com/research/report/corporate-venture-capital-trends-q3-2022: Last accessed 06-Oct-2022.
4. Startup Stash, "Top 25 Angel Investing Tools/Platforms," URL: https://startupstash.com/angel-investing-tools: Last accessed 06-Oct-2022.
5. Nathan Reiff, "Series Funding: A, B, and C," Investopedia, 24-Feb-2022, URL: https://www.investopedia.com/articles/personal-finance/102015/series-b-c-funding-what-it-all-means-and-how-it-works.asp Last Accessed: 01-Oct-2022.
6. Alex Iskold, 9 Personal and Painful Reasons why Founders do not get the investment, URL: https://www.startuphacks.vc/blog/2019/07/16/9-personal-and-painful-reasons-why-founders-do-not-get-the-investment last accessed 24-Sep-2022
7. Fundz, "Series A, B, C Funding: Averages, Investors, Valuations," URL: https://www.fundz.net/what-is-series-a-funding-series-b-funding-and-more: Last accessed 01-Oct-2022. I may need to change this reference, as it has some errors.
8. Aswath Damodaran, "Venture Capital: It is a pricing, not a value, game!" Musings on Markets, 02-Oct-2016, URL: https://aswathdamodaran.blogspot.com/2016/10/venture-capital-it-is-pricing-not-value.html: Last accessed 01-Sep-

2022.

9. Prof. Aswath Damodaran, "Valuing Young Companies," https://www.youtube.com/watch?v=CgtGKRQzLyU (last accessed 01-Sep-2022). Prof. Damodaran presents the valuation of Amazon in detail as an early-stage firm with early revenues.
10. James Dargan, "21 of the World's Top Quantum Investors in 2022," The Quantum Insider, 08-Jun-2022, URL: https://thequantuminsider.com/2022/06/08/quantum-investors: Last accessed: 01-Oct-2022.
11. Crunchbase, Magic Leap, https://www.crunchbase.com/organization/magic-leap last accessed 01-Apr-2022.
12. Heather Somerville, "Investors Pour Into Venture Capital Funds Even as Markets Cool," The Wall Street Journal, 02-Nov-2022, https://www.wsj.com/articles/venture-capital-stays-hot-with-investors-even-as-markets-cool-11667357577: Last accessed 06-Nov-2022.
13. Chris Dixon, "The Idea Maze," 04-Aug-2018, URL: https://cdixon.org/2013/08/04/the-idea-maze: Last accessed 01-Oct-2022.
14. Salesflare, "The Ultimate Term Sheet Guide – all terms and clauses explained," URL: https://blog.salesflare.com/term-sheet-guide: Last accessed 01-Oct-2022.
15. Akhilesh Ganti, "Term Sheets: Definition, What's Included, Examples, and Key Terms," Investopedia, last updated: 28-Aug-2022, URL: https://www.investopedia.com/terms/t/termsheet.asp, Last accessed 01-Oct-2022.
16. Legasis Partners, "Decoding the Liquidation Preference Clause in Investment Transactions," 01-Jun-2019, URL: https://www.legallyindia.com/private-equity-unleashed/decoding-the-liquidation-preference-clause-in-investment-transactions-20190601-11012. Last accessed: 01-Oct-2022

17. Brad Feld, "To Participate or Not (Participating Preferences,)" 24-Aug-2004, URL: https://feld.com/archives/2004/08/to-participate-or-not-participating-preferences: Last accessed 01-Oct-2022.

THE PATH TO GREATNESS IS ROUGH

Fight one more round. When your feet are so tired that you have to shuffle back to the center of the ring, fight one more round. When your arms are so tired that you can hardly lift your hands to come on guard, fight one more round. When your nose is bleeding, and your eyes are black, and you are so tired you wish your opponent would crack you one on the jaw and put you to sleep, fight one more round – remembering that the man who always fights one more round is never whipped.

– James J. Corbett (1), American Professional Boxer (2)

BEFORE YOU START

Naren was very fortunate to get some time with the legendary CEO, with whom he had developed acquaintance years back from an airplane conversation. This industry leader CEO had built a billion-dollar firm from the ground up and is now successfully growing it to the sky. Naren was ready to pitch his idea, but the CEO interrupted him and said he instead gave some helpful advice before Naren started his startup. Naren found most of the advice to be superficial, and "common knowledge." The conversation sounded impressive, but, Naren didn't perceive any actionable. After two years, now Naren's firm is in trouble. He felt he should have listened better. Why does it happen? Why do founders tend to ignore the advice they hear from those who have been there and done that? For many first-time founders, the startup is a passionate love affair. *Startups are counterintuitive.* Knowledge about building startups is slow to permeate into our system. Our gut feelings and intuitions only work sometimes. The advice feels unnecessary, occasionally strenuous to execute (e.g., customer discovery, market opportunity navigator) and clumsy to do before it becomes a habit. You get impatient and are likely to skip the advice. Our intuition develops based on our experiences in life. Our intuition is likely correct in assessing technology trends if we have had that experience. But in unfamiliar situations that arise in a startup, it is better to seek advisors, learn from masterclasses, critically analyze available data, and not rely on gut feeling. Understanding all aspects and mechanics of building a startup or learning from anecdotes can only give you a few perspectives. Learning "tricks" doesn't work most often.

Eventually, you must make a product or service that users want. You know this when growth is not the firm's most significant problem but keeping up and delivering to the demand.

BUILDING A FIRM IS TO CAUSE A METAMORPHOSIS

Metamorphosis is a striking change in an organism's form, structure, and behavior. Life starts as an egg and progresses through larva, pupa, and finally, the butterfly! The organism's physical appearance, food, to behavior change through the phases. Complete metamorphosis is the extreme transformation of the firm. And the metamorphosis of the founder precedes the firm. Founders who are not interested or capable of such a transformation usually take an exit at a stage and start again with the next innovation.

All living beings are continuously self-creating. Cells in the human body lives for a few hours to seven years, utmost. All thriving firms are like living beings. They are self-creating. Firms are living systems with the team members continuously changing. They go through metamorphosis and renewal as they mature.

FOUNDING A FIRM IS INVENTING A BUSINESS MODEL

It all starts with a crucial problem to solve—a widely experienced problem, i.e., the solution is likely to have a significant market opportunity. You must begin exploring the problem using first principles to discover the fundamental needs and wants of the customer. During this process, explore if there is economic value in solving the problem—can we make money? If the idea is about making a social impact, there is low possibility of making money directly from the beneficiary. In that case, figuring out an economic model to sustain the venture is essential. And contemplate what you must do to exploit the opportunity before investing in building the solution. It doesn't need much financial capital to make progress validating before you build the product.

Successful founders are *optimistic skeptics*. The transition from an innovator to an entrepreneur is about humility. Will customers care or value my idea? Can I build a working business model? Do I have evidence of progress in the real world than in my imagination? And they develop a process to adapt their idea ("pivot") until customers value it, and a thriving business model emerges. It is about *inventing a business model*, which is different from management—it is exploration.

Mature companies can be as innovative as startups if they internalize this process of *founding a business*. They could do it even better because they have access to customers, financial and other resources. Modern enterprises innovate with a tool chest of different processes: open innovation, collaboration with startups as peer mentors and early adopters, investing (corporate venture capital,) and M&A.

Business leaders of mature enterprises undergoing digital transformation or diversification to innovation-led new business opportunities empower innovators as *intrapreneurs* to lead new business initiatives. They avoid directing the intrapreneur with their solutions but provide *inputs, coaching, and advice* that the intrapreneur is free to take after due consideration. Such empowered intrapreneurial leaders produce exceptional results for the enterprise.

Scaling up the firm beyond PMF takes management. Many technologists and engineers nurture a dislike of the idea of *management*. Let's face it, scaling up the team precedes the firm's growth. Scaling a company is only about management and how much the founder is willing to develop their management competence.

HOW YOU HANDLE YOUR SUCCESS MATTERS MOST

We have all heard the maxim, "Failure is the steppingstone to success." We also know the story of a spider's attempts to build its web, inspiring King Bruce to win his empire by fighting many battles. While this maxim applies at the basic level, entrepreneurship calls for good judgment to change the business strategy to succeed with a reasonable amount of time and capital. It would help if you built viable stepping stones toward the outcomes that indicate success.

We can learn by observing hugely successful and impactful entrepreneurs about how they handled their setbacks. Of course, their lives show how hard it was for them to overcome failures and rejections. But they were also glaring examples of how they handled their small successes with humility such that they could reach the greatest of successes they ultimately attained. Many entrepreneurs fail to scale their businesses because they stop scaling themselves up after a few initial successes—securing initial funding, achieving a thriving position in the industry, etc.

WE CAN GET SMART TO CREATE LUCK

You may fail to scale and grow your firm even with the best efforts. One firm may be lucky to close its equity funding just a few days before the market crash after the 911 attack, a financial market crash, or the pandemic. In contrast, many others lost opportunities due to a crisis beyond their control. We hear numerous exciting stories of how someone got lucky. Let us use "serendipity" to stand for "luck, divine intervention, mere statistical probability, etc." Serendipity is consistently associated with unexpected and positive personal events that accelerate your business, inventions, and discoveries that become disproportionately valuable. After all, entrepreneurship is a matter of serendipity and conversations. US President Obama once said, *"There was this element of chance to it—this element of serendipity,"* when he spoke about his success.

Success happens when preparedness meets opportunity and potentiality. Ultimately, it is the combination of competence and luck that creates superlative success, not luck alone. Developing competence is, therefore, the starting point.

On one of his business trips, Naren happened to sit next to a business leader unknown to him. By the end of the trip, Naren had won a long-term customer relationship for his firm. This could only have happened if Naren had taken the initiative to open a conversation with his co-passenger and had the preparedness to deliver the value the customer was looking for. Unless you try to connect, potentiality cannot happen. It would help if you increased your odds. It would be best if you built your preparedness to benefit from serendipity. You cannot anticipate the situations that would happen to you randomly. But *you can pick your response.* That leads to what we call luck or serendipity over a period. It is essential to distinguish between *blind luck* (e.g., where you are born) and *smart luck* that you can work to create.

Practice including a *hook* in your conversations that can generate interest in the other person. For instance, instead of introducing yourself just factually, try adding a hook statement the listener might respond to (your *one-line value proposition.*) For example, *"Our firm improves yield in solar panel manufacturing."*

There are natural advantages or constraints of the environment you choose to operate in. For instance, Silicon Valley is the most favorable environment for DeepTech ventures. And there are self-limiting beliefs (e.g., fear of rejection) or assumptions (e.g., big companies will not work with startups) that you must overcome, by creating a new experience.

HOW LONG TO PERSEVERE?

When an entrepreneur succeeds, not just one person succeeds but a community and society. First, the successful entrepreneur causes many offspring founders and causes a chain reaction of wealth creation. It is good for your community, country, and the world. So, aim high. You may be the chosen one to make that difference. The main problem we often face is not that we aim too high and fail, but we aim too low and succeed. This is the situation with many thriving MSME firms.

Perseverance is a virtue of successful entrepreneurs. But it is not being in denial. When the evidence is against the assumption, it is time to downsize, save capital, or even shutdown altogether. Persevere only if you acknowledge the reality and there is an alternate path.

Entrepreneurship is lonely, even though you have many companions on the journey. Continuously develop an attitude of recovery from setbacks, lifelong learning, and humility. You must quit the venture if your idea is not gaining customers, even after multiple pivots. If you feel, "No one seems to get this; I am ahead of time," it is time to give up. Inspirational quotes about "believing in yourself and keep going" are applicable in a specific context. *Always have an outer limit timeline and budget plan to exit before you start.*

LIVE TO FIGHT ANOTHER DAY

Most ventures fail to generate revenue and economic value. Your firm may fall into a chasm as you toil the climb. Founders could get emotionally attached to the firm and may tend to finance it themselves, digging into their savings to "keep it going." Passionate founders will continue investing time and money. Consider this carefully, and never over-invest your personal wealth into your venture. Borrowing money personally to invest in your venture can be suicidal and can shut all your opportunities to create another firm in your life. Building a scalable firm fast takes substantial capital at high risk. So, get others to fund your venture—you can learn how to raise funding, or drive it slow to take off exponential. Getting other stakeholders will most likely save you from falling over the cliff. If you don't want to raise funding, then practice with a lifestyle business or bootstrap and grow your firm by reinvesting profits. Most firms in the world do not receive any venture capital.

You either succeed as an entrepreneur, or you don't. There is no consolation prize in this game. Neither should you accept any consolation—it is worthless. Be wise to exit early and live to fight another day. You deserve to succeed, after all, once an entrepreneur, always an entrepreneur. Living with an entrepreneurial spirit and a broken back is the worst thing to happen to anyone. So, stay fit to fight one more round.

There is no smooth road to the heights of greatness. The path is rough, and you must trek it with training and the help of many Sherpas. It is a journey in search of yourself; it is worth the toil. Let me conclude quoting the wisdom from Dr. G. Venkataswamy, founder of Aravind Eye Care System (Aravind.org), a world-class eye care institution: *"Intelligence and capability are not enough. There must be the joy of doing something beautiful."*

KEY TAKEAWAYS AND ACTION PLANNING

1) The essential elements presented to technologists for building innovation-led firms are:
   a) Augment intuition with deliberation: test your assumptions with evidence, or *evidence-based intuitive entrepreneurship*.
   b) Progress from foresight to forecast; practice forward-looking reviews, to sharpen forecasts.
   c) Build interdependent, complimenting team.
   d) Balance focus and agility.
   e) Optimize capital.
2) Develop a deep knowledge of your customer and market, and

strive to build a product that customers want and firm customers love.
3) Continuously develop an attitude of recovery from setbacks, lifelong learning, and humility.
4) Have an outer limit timeline and budget plan to exit before you start. Don't overinvest in your venture.
5) Strive to build an institution that strives to create economic and social value for people. Let there be the joy of doing something beautiful.

CALL TO ACTION

1. Browse the list of curated resources at the end of this book and familiarize yourself with a set of resources that will be relevant to you in different stages of developing your venture.
2. Consider becoming part of an incubator cohort especially when you are a first-time entrepreneur.

REFERENCES

1. https://en.wikipedia.org/wiki/James_J._Corbett accessed on 30-Jul-2022

https://www.goodreads.com/quotes/540142-fight-one-more-round-when-your-feet-are-so-tired

APPENDIX-1

TERMINOLOGY IN THIS BOOK

Capital: Wealth and assets used to generate more wealth or assets. Assets produce future income (cash flows.) In the context of technology-based ventures, capital, and assets can be monetary, physical (tangible,) or intellectual (intangible.)

Capitalism: The essential feature of capitalism is the motive to profit in a competitive environment, creative destruction (1), with private ownership of capital and profits. Freedom of trade, voluntary exchange, and the rule of law are essential to capitalism and entrepreneurship. Founders need to internalize how this economic system of capitalism works, as it sets the rules of the game of entrepreneurship. A growing number of business leaders act based on the belief that business is about *more* than making a profit; it is about a higher purpose. Founders inclined to that belief are invited to read more about *Conscious Capitalism* (2). In human existence, *value extraction* is rewarded more than *value creation*—the creative, inventive, productive process. Those who want to develop a deeper understanding of extracting value through an innovation economy, please read (3).

Chief Financial Officer (CFO): CFO is a corporate job title for the senior-most executive in a firm's management team responsible for managing the company's financial operations and strategy. In this book, we use the term *good CFO* to represent advisors, consultants, and professional service providers who counsel the founder / CEO on finance, governance, administration, compliance, and legal aspects of operating the firm and making decisions that have profound implications.

Co-founder: Lead employees who work directly with the Founder in the startup team as co-owners of the *firm*.

Consumer: User of the product or service--they consume. Consumers may not pay for the product; they may be beneficiaries. The one who pays the firm is the *Customer*, who may also be the consuming beneficiary.

Client: The client is a customer who purchases professional services from the firm. Most often, clients buy *solutions*. Clients are also more loyal to the firm than customers and spend more money with the firm. The firm must strive to develop long-term relationships with clients. This book uses the term customer to stand for clients as well.

Company: A company is a legal entity formed by individuals to engage in and operate a business enterprise in a commercial or industrial capacity (4). In this book, we use the terms "Company" and "Firm" (see below) synonymously.

Customer: The *customer* buys products or services from the firm. In the context of this book, the Customer pays for the firm's product. This term is used in this book to stand for all kinds of revenue sources for the firm, such as paying consumers (B2C, D2C) business entities (B2B,) and clients. Customers acknowledge the problem you are solving for them and are willing and able to pay for the *solution* that solves the problem (or meets the need.)

DeepTech (or **Hardtech**): Startups that are characterized by predominantly higher **technology risk** (*"Can we build it?"*) and **capital risk** (*"How can we find the capital to build it?"*). When successfully overcoming the technical risk and building the product, such a firm will likely have a large addressable market. They combine fundamental technology development in the context of commercial pragmatism. DeepTech firms provide solutions based on substantial scientific or engineering advances. Such firms build a new capability that did not exist before and therefore are supported by significant intellectual property assets. DeepTech firms are high on *scientific novelty*, and the addressable market must be carefully assessed to establish viability and scalability. DeepTech companies work in the earlier phase technology revolution framework, and they are characterized by *technology push*. The most significant risk with DeepTech companies is their timing and opportunity to monetize the fundamental inventions.

Have you heard of General Magic (5)? If you haven't, please *Google* it.

DigitalTech: In this book, the term *DigitalTech* is used to stand for all the businesses that are powered by emerging digital technology—computing, communication, audio/video, web (delivery models such as Software-as-a-Service, Internet-of-Things,) artificial intelligence, machine learning, blockchain, virtual reality, 3D printing and so on. DigitalTech firms create new user experiences with dramatic efficiency improvements at a larger scale of operation, transforming existing processes and business models to create economic growth. We hear about these firms as fintech, mobility tech, retail tech, logistics tech, MedTech, health tech, agri-tech, reg-tech, legal tech, etc. These firms *deploy* the technology, and such innovation opportunity is enormous at the beginning of every technological revolution. The "tech" identity is transitory until the new business system becomes *ubiquitous*.

Traditional firms that transform and transition their business using digital technology survive when the transformation is complete. DigitalTech firms are not necessarily DeepTech firms, as they may not invent new technologies to build their service or solution. They integrate emerging technology components to solve a significant customer problem, building an innovative *system*. Most DigitalTech firms are characterized by **market risk** (*"Will people buy it?"*) and

execution risk (*"Can we scale this firm?"*).

DigitalTech firms are typically low or medium on scientific novelty but have a large addressable market. A few firms start as DigitalTech firms and transform into DeepTech firms as they grow (e.g., Amazon.) Most DigitalTech startup firms end up being low market size. They can scale up and survive if they manage their business model well to be sustainably profitable.

Entrepreneur: See, *Founder*.

Expansion: Improving the firms reach (e.g., expanding to a new geo region), increasing production capacity (e.g., new factory) and resources. Expansion is more easily understood and executed than *scaling up*. Therefore, most entrepreneurs mature their firms as SMEs and do not aspire to scaleup.

Founder: The primary entrepreneur who leads the development of the idea into a firm or institution that is viable and sustainable for the long term. In the context of this book, co-founders who join in supporting the primary founder's vision with substantial compensation in equity are also included, even though they are *entrepreneurial employees*.

Firm: Commercial entity (vehicle) that undertakes the journey of building economic value from innovation. The term *firm* is preferred in this book instead of the equivalent popular terms such as business, company, organization, etc., to link the concept with the microeconomic theory (6) and associated body of work.

Growth: Increasing externally influenced results (outcomes) for the firm—revenue, profits, customer loyalty, etc.

Intrapreneur: Employee entrepreneur within the scope of an established business, mainly compensated in salary and incentives, and sometimes small equity stake. In the context of this book, the term founder includes intrapreneurs too. See, *Founder*.

Journey: Metaphor to describe the development of an idea into a particular product or service by a *firm* and used by *Customers*. This book concerns, for the most part, a single product or service that starts as an idea in someone's mind. This book focuses on the early journey from the idea to a *thriving* firm.

Product (vs. Service): In the context of this book, the term product is also used to represent a service product.

Scale: Improve activity level, capability, and productivity. Scale takes the capital efficiency into consideration and related to the business model.

Scaleup: A firm that is in the process of stepping up its capabilities and capacity to grow results rapidly. When a firm has achieved initial product-market fit, it is ready to scale up and achieves the scaleup stage when it establishes business model fit. Beyond this point adding resources could take the firm to the thriving stage rapidly.

Solution: A solution is an implementation to solve one or more problems, combining people, processes, insights and products/services in a distinct system [adapted from Gartner Technology Glossary.]

Startup: A temporary organization in search of establishing a repeatable, scalable, and sustainable business model. When a founder has evidence for problem-solution fit starting from an idea, it is the right time to form a startup. Technology development and customer discovery are ideally completed before starting up. A business venture that has no technology or innovation (e.g., trading, distribution) or no ambition or plan to rapidly grow to address a large market (e.g., a neighborhood restaurant, professional services firm) are *new business ventures*; no appropriate to be called startups.

Value *(n)*: Economic value is a measure of the benefit a product or service provides to the beneficiary who receives the benefit, measured in currency units. It is not the same as the (market) *price* or *market value*. Consumer exchanges price for value. Value is a deep economic concept, and it is associated with tangible and intangible properties.

Value *(v)*: the process of assessing the value of an object or entity.

Value Chain: It is the model of all activities and contributing entities to deliver a specific benefit (product or service) to a beneficiary. Typically, each contributing entity adds value to the final product/service.

Value Creation: Firms that grow and earn a return on capital that exceeds their cost of capital create economic value.

Venture: To venture is to proceed despite the risk of failure or danger. And venture is an initiative that is inherently risky about the outcome. Ventures aspire to produce a profit or create a positive social impact (not-for-profit.) In either case, *creating sustainable economic value* is the venture's goal.

REFERENCES

1. Joseph A. Schumpeter, "Capitalism, Socialism and Democracy," 3rd edition, Harper Perennial Modern Thought edition, 2008, ISBN 978-0-06-156161-0, pp. 81-86.
2. John Mackey and Rajendra Sisodia, "Conscious Capitalism," 2014, Harvard Business Review Press, ISBN 978-1-62527-175-4.
3. Mariana Mazzucato, "The Value of Everything: Making and Taking in the Global Economy," Allen Lane, Penguin Random House UK, 2018, ISBN 978-0-241-34779-9, pp. 6-8, pp.189-228.
4. What Is a Company, How to Start One, Different Types, Investopedia, https://www.investopedia.com/terms/c/company.asp: last accessed 01-Sep-2022.
5. Google, v. An example of technology becoming part of our lingo.
6. Daniel F. Spulber, "The Theory of the Firm: Microeconomics with Endogenous Entrepreneurs, Firms, Markets, and Organizations," Cambridge University Press, ISBN 978-0-521-51738-6, 2009.

APPENDIX-2

PREPARING FOR INVESTOR INTERACTION

One critical to success competency for the founder/CEO is effectively interacting with investors and bankers if you intend to build and operate the firm raising external capital. Realize that you must prepare for interaction and conversation with your firm's most critical future partners, the *capital providers*. Venture Capital (VC) firms typically do not want to get operationally involved in the firms they invest in. However, specific VCs would be willing to facilitate new business relationships or even step in to perform operational roles in *ad interim*.

WHERE TO GET CAPITAL FROM?

Customers are the best source of capital. Funding product development (or the *non-recurring engineering costs*) using customer advance payments is the best option every DeepTech or DigitalTech firm must strive for. If the value proposition is sufficiently robust and solves a significant customer problem, it is easier to implement this strategy.

Re-investing profits from a thriving venture to create a new venture is the best way to develop the firm as a valuable enterprise. Several tech firms have successfully implemented this strategy, even though the process requires a lot of patience and discipline to build growth systematically over decades.

The next best source of capital in the startup's initial days is your investments from your family and friends or individuals who trust you. Be extremely careful and deliberate about using any of these options, as the likelihood of losing all that money is near 100% at the early stages of any venture, you could end up losing close and affectionate relationships.

A wiser option is to seek contest prizes, equity-free grants, or grants from the Government and Corporate sources through incubators, accelerators, etc. Don't waste time in the initial days seeking awards that do not come with substantial prize money!

Suppliers/Partners may also have ways to fund your venture if they can relate to the benefits they could draw from your successful execution. For instance, many cloud providers offer startups monetary credit for using their infrastructure. However, the terms of engagement are essential to comprehend before signing up. Receiving equity investment from Suppliers or Customers, can lead to conflicts and complexities hard to manage.

Many investors, especially incubators/accelerators, offer *convertible debenture* instruments for investments in very early stage ventures. This mechanism helps to sidestep the complex negotiation of valuation. Please comprehend the terms carefully with the help of a *good CFO*.

Several new-age financial services firms are willing to provide working capital loans against early revenues the startup firm has achieved. Conventional loans from Banks or financial institutions are feasible only when your firm has achieved predictable revenues. Pledging your personal assets to raise a loan for your firm is not wise.

Please read the following sections if you decide to proceed with equity financing. Request your accounting team to prepare for the *due diligence* of your firm. This would mean preparing financial and legal data in an organized manner for external auditors or assessors to examine easily.

MAKE INFORMED DECISIONS ON EQUITY FINANCING

Many venture capital firms are in different shapes and sizes, and the subject matter is vast, complicated, and complex. The subject matter is founded on economics and secondary school mathematics at scale. Financing or investment is an industry with some of the most intelligent people working. All founders must develop an appreciation for the subject matter and understand the fundamentals before starting to raise venture capital. You can neither afford to ignore this subject nor develop deep expertise. This chapter explains a few concepts and nuances of raising equity financing, and the aim is to sensitize and prepare you to raise capital. This is not professional or legal advice. We barely scratch the surface here.

Several excellent books are available covering this essential topic. To better understand the subject, here are three books curated for you (1) (2) (3). It would be best to rely on professional help from your good CFO besides books, blog articles, conferences, webinars, etc., while making crucial decisions regarding accepting equity investment. It is also wise not to waste time learning about *"fundraising."* Instead, if you build a valuable firm, and take the support of experienced advisors, investors will find you.

THINKING ABOUT YOUR PITCH DECK

The founder must prepare three distinct "pitch" decks targeted to three audiences, who all have other alternatives.

1. Customer: How do we help you fulfill your JTBD?
2. Employee: Why should you be part of this journey?
3. Investor: Why should you invest in our firm?

This section concerns only the investor. It is best you attempt making the investor pitch only after you prepare the pitch for customers and employees.

You will find hundreds of lovely templates and examples of legendary investor pitch decks in a jiffy with a Google search. However, most technologist founders need help making their investor pitch (not just a pitch deck) and getting rightly oriented to perform this crucial role effectively. Please read Chapter 10 before you start to make your pitch.

1. A strategic thinking and resource planning process leads you to the investor pitch deck. It narrates the future history of your firm as you envision it. It must convey a story supported by trackable numbers and facts (verifiable story.) The hero in the story is the *customer*, and the villain is the *problem* that bothers the customer. Your firm provides the *weapon* for the hero to vanquish the villain.
2. Strategic thinking precedes fundraising preparation. Make a detailed diagnosis of the current state and establish the strategic objective to be achieved in 18 and 36 months in terms of outcomes for the firm. The key results are externally recognizable evidence for progress against your hypotheses. You must prepare to answer the investor's question on how the funds will be used. It is best to specify the use of funds in terms of outcomes (e.g., expanding from the current X customers to Y customers) and not actions or outputs (e.g., hiring a sales team.) The resource plan (or use of funds) shows your preparation to produce outcomes. The RFF associated with this strategic vision would show the fund requirements and deduce from that the long-term investment and short-term working capital requirements (based on the cash flow statement.)
3. Early-stage investors (individuals, accelerators, and angel investor funds) want to see proof of executing the value proposition through early revenue or other evidence of execution. Letter of Intent, MoUs, paid PoCs, etc., are reasonable evidence of progress when revenue is yet to start. Analysis of customer interviews and learning from them,

detailed estimation of Customer lifetime value (LTV), Customer Acquisition Cost (CAC), etc., are interesting for investors to comprehend the business model.
4. The first significant milestone goal for all startups is to achieve PMF. When a company is nearing PMF, the critical indicators are (a) Gross Margins achieved, (b) NPS, Customer retention, and (c) the quantum of incoming new customer leads via referrals and marketing efforts.
5. Strategic investors (corporates, individual investors) are appropriate when the factor limiting your growth is something money can't buy (e.g., market access to a country, integration with a critical complementary value proposition.) Strategic investors can relate to your firm's business challenges and the market space you are operating in. The strategic value the investor brings to the business is more important than the monetary value of the investment. Understanding and accommodating the strategic investor's investment goals is fundamental before accepting the investment.
6. Usually, a combination of enormous market opportunity and ease of executing the business against that market opportunity is a point of interest to investors. From the market perspective, you must have a clear logic to explain how the outcomes would differ with and without funding. Will this investment accelerate your results? For instance, entering the US market now versus three years later or completing clinical trials for the medical device.
7. Plan your startup's milestones as externally influenced events (e.g., design win for your chip, first paid PoC signup, or 1,000 downloads, crossing 50 customers) that are easily recognized. These are the business outcomes the startup must aim for and plan. While internal milestones (e.g., hiring the 100th employee, MVP launch, product launch) help plan the spending, they must correlate with achieving market results. These milestones are only relevant to writing

the company's history when it is successful.
8. Classify the capital required into two categories. *Long-term investment* is to create assets and build capability to produce future revenues. Short-term capital or *working capital* is the money required to deliver against customer demand, or to generate the revenue. The strategy to secure and manage these two types of capital must be different. *Capital allocation and optimization* is a crucial skill founder/CEO must learn and develop.

Pitch Deck Guidelines

All investors are seeking answers to the following questions.

1. *Is there a significant market opportunity?* (Is there an acute problem to be solved in the world? Will the solution to the problem likely yield money?)
2. *How lucrative is this market opportunity?* (Is there money to be made? What is the profitability characteristic?)
3. *Why is this team the right one to win this opportunity?*

Your messaging to the investor must provide answers to all three questions convincingly. Please note that the first two questions are independent of your firm.

1. We must prepare an *elevator pitch* and three (sometimes four) types of pitch decks. If needed, you must get professional help to prepare them elegantly—no spelling errors, large-sized fonts with contrasting colors, etc. These documents need not be artistic works of art. Just easy to read on a small form factor mobile screen.
    a) **Elevator pitch**: This is the shortest communication version of your firm. Elevator pitch is delivered/spoken in meetings and other social occasions, formal or casual. It must be

worded accordingly to flow well and easily understood. You must memorize it and rehearse it several times to get it right. No slides. Your talk shall not exceed a short "elevator ride" of 20 to 30 seconds. You must prepare 2-3 minutes expanded version too. The audience for the elevator pitch is neutral—customers, employees, other stakeholders and investors. It would be best to leave the audience excited and curious to learn more. The elevator pitch is the most distilled form of communication, ideally prepared last in every iteration of preparing the communication about your firm

b) **Intro deck** or *email deck*: one for the email to get a meeting (ideally nine or fewer slides); this is essentially an advertisement seeking investor attention—its purpose is to arouse curiosity to meet with you, and the outcome is an appointment with the investor. Nothing more. For compelling reasons, if you must have more slides, never more than fifteen, or make it as a short video. Create a communication meant for investors as the audience, and recipients read this deck or watch a short video.

c) **Meeting deck**: You will use this deck to present your firm in the first investor meeting (for supporting *your presentation for about 18 minutes* or less.) Prepare this deck to prompt your presentation flow. If you got only 3 minutes or less with the audience, what would you tell them? Make that the first couple of minutes of content. Use this part for pitch events too. What if you got another 3 minutes? Make that the next set of content. Each segment must arouse the curiosity to listen more from you. If you can demonstrate the product, show samples, etc., it should be part of this presentation within this time. You could embed the demo anywhere in the presentation if you can present it without losing the flow and tempo for the audience. Ideally, have recorded demos or videos of field trials etc. Leave ample time for interaction and discussions. Rehearsing is essential—zoom talk, in person, etc. Record your pitch and watch it later to discover improvement opportunities. This deck is not meant for emailing and make it creative and attractive to support your delivery style.

d) **Information deck:** If your first meeting went well, the investors would ask you to share more information. This deck is meant to provide more details of your strategic narrative supported by RFF summary for 3-5 years. Before you share this, you must have done some due diligence about the investor and be interested in bringing them as a partner to your firm. Share these details only with short-listed investors after the meeting for reading/reference preferably under a non-disclosure agreement (NDA.) Beware, almost no investor agrees to sign NDA at this stage. Therefore, the content must be carefully planned. This deck will be more factual (market spaces, assumptions, risks, etc.) and numbers (financial, market sizing, etc.)

e) **Information Memo**: This document captures the detailed narrative about the firm's business model and plans and the workings of financial projections. Usually a running document, not a presentation deck. It is an excellent practice to prepare the info memo as a living document to develop clarity for the startup. It is a good practice to model the info memo around *red herring prospectus (RHP)* of larger firms in a similar domain, especially the market space analysis, risk disclosures, and firm's strategy/operating plan. Studying RHPs of firms in your domain would greatly help you develop the lingo to communicate with investors.

2. Starting with the Info Memo and working backward to the elevator pitch makes it easier to get the flow right. Adapting the presentation deck depending on the audience profile and what you learn from interactions is good. *Simplicity comes out of deep understanding.* You must first prepare detailed information oriented to the investors. Then extract the shorter content from it for the different decks.

3. Prepare the Info Memo as a running text (e.g., Microsoft Word or Google document) capturing the details of the narrative of your business. Following the language and structure of RHP, except the legal and financial parts, would help create an investor-friendly communication. This is the narrative's detailed script, which numbers (financial and non-financial) and pieces of evidence (facts) must support. Make this your working document to share with your key team members and investors. Once this document is final, you can start preparing the presentations. *If this document is the movie script, the elevator pitch and the first pitch deck are trailers.*

4. Start with an unambiguous problem statement (what is the problem we are solving?), and explain why it is urgent to solve it now (present evidence for this.) Who has this problem and is pained by it (ideal customer prospect, ICP)? How have you established it (data needed)? How big is that ICP population? Essentially, this section focuses on the demand characteristics of your firm.

5. Present your solution: What is your solution to the abovementioned problem? Cover and prove your unique insights and how it solves the problem you said. Any evidence that your solution works? What is differentiated and/or unique about your solution? Demonstrate how you

would gain customer acceptance of the solution compared to the alternatives they may have today. If you had any early customers, talk about them now.

6. In the case of slide decks 2 and 3, you will plant a short video or recorded demo showing your superior customer experience use case. Show how your solution will solve the problem you stated.

7. Business Development and Go-to-Market strategy: Show your understanding of your customers and prioritize a plan of action for those customer segments. Explain your logic of choice (business strategy.)

8. Now present the market space details: Classify the market opportunities for your technology and product based on potential and *your challenges* to realize that potential. Choose the one market opportunity you are pursuing now, and your growth (if it succeeds) and backup (if it fails) options. Calculate your total addressable market (TAM) bottom-up, not top-down—i.e., starting from your unit pricing, and expand to your market space (ideal customer profile, additional customers.) Calculate the serviceable obtainable market (SOM) first based on your estimated number of customers/transactions in a year multiplied by your unit price. Similarly, serviceable addressable market (SAM) and TAM. Most founders fail to present credible market size estimations of SOM-SAM-TAM with a clear roadmap. Show how you arrived at the numbers. Have you verified it? You could present separate market size estimates for the growth and backup options. For instance you may be challenged to address large enterprises due to lack of relationships. This challenge may be overcome almost instantly by adding an appropriate leader to the team.

9. Competitive Landscape: Present as a table starting with your prioritized, measurable customer *benefits* (not features) and competitors' position.

10. Projected Financials: mention your approach to financial

planning and the accuracy estimate. Remember, no one expects you to be right 100% at this stage. Relate the numbers to your strategic narrative. For instance, if you plan to expand to a new geo, show the investments and spend for that plan clearly.

11. The investor wants to know how you have considered the assumptions/risks and plan to manage them. Show Unit economics, Gross Margins, EBITDA, Net Profit, Cash flow, and RoCE over three years (5 years for late revenue starters such as DeepTech or more evolved firms.) Specifically mention your revenue parameters—e.g., in the case of a SaaS company, run rate must include only the subscription revenue; show other one-time revenues, if any, as separate revenue streams.

12. Capital being asked: Investors invest for returns and seek evidence that indicate future returns. Your investor pitch should, therefore, communicate the use of funds linked to outcomes and not spend heads. For e.g., instead of saying, "need 100K to build engineering team," mention what outcome the engineering team could produce with 100K, such as "scale the product to serve 1M users." Link capital to the outcome (milestones, benefits investors can relate to) you seek to achieve with the money (not the number of months of runway.) If your business will require more money to be raised after this, provide the indications. For instance, in the case of a medical device product, the primary fundraising milestones can be *clinical trials, certifications, manufacturing readiness, market launch,* and so on.

13. Intellectual Property (IP) Strategy: Rather than merely listing the patents and associated status present their relevance to the value proposition and commercialization options. The genesis of the patents, especially those that originated from solving a real customer problem, indicate higher market value. Is there potential to license the technology & patent rights to other firms, or are these

defensive patents? By the same token, is your firm likely to face patent infringement risks when it starts to grow revenues? IP strategy is essential for DeepTech firms.
14. Team: This slide aims to establish a team capable of executing the above plan—*why are we in the best position to solve this problem?* Explain the individuals' role in the firm now and establish their credibility in the context. What is the relevant previous experience or inspiration to execute the plan? Beyond the co-founders, show prominent part-time members, partners signed up, advisors, board, etc.—and delineate them accordingly.
15. Technical architecture overview—single slide version of the technology architecture components, etc. Simplify the representation so that someone without any technical background can get an idea about the unique aspects of your solution. If this slide kindles interest in learning more about your solution, it serves its purpose. You could avoid this and expect the investor to ask for it.
16. Purpose, Mission, Vision, Values: How do you visualize your firm for 3-5 years (max seven years)? How would the industry look then, and how would your company have a dominant position? This is an essential part of employee pitch deck, but avoidable for the investors, unless they ask for it.

BE PREPARED FOR GRUELING NEGOTIATION

Be mentally prepared to be in long grueling meetings and stressful situations until the investment process is completed. The definition of "done" is when the first tranche of investment money is received in your firm's bank account. Remember, the asymmetry in the relationship. Investors negotiate as part of their profession. Before starting the negotiation, determine the minimum terms you're willing to accept. Take active support and advice from the *good CFO*. Let's face it, no negotiation will ever be perfect. There will always be some give and take. And you will develop the muscles too, step by step. Always be respectful, listen carefully, and avoid making any emotional appeals.

FOR FURTHER READING

1. Brad Feld and Jason Mendelson, "Venture Deals: Be Smarter Than Your Lawyer and Venture Capitalist," 4th Edition, Wiley, 2019, Kindle Edition.
2. Gordon Daugherty, "Startup Success: Funding the Early Stages of Your Venture," River Grove Books, 2019, Kindle Edition.

REFERENCES

1. Saurabh Jain, "Startup Masterclass: Guide for Startup Founders," fun2do Labs, 2022.
2. Brad Feld and Jason Mendelson, "Venture Deals: Be Smarter Than Your Lawyer and Venture Capitalist," 4th Edition, Amazon Kindle Edition, Wiley, 2019.
3. William H. Draper III, "The Startup Game: Inside the Partnership between Venture Capitalists and Entrepreneurs," Amazon Kindle Edition, St. Martin's Press, 2011.

Insert chapter ten text here. Insert chapter ten text here. Insert chapter ten text here. Insert chapter ten text here. Insert chapter ten text here. Insert chapter ten text here. Insert chapter ten text here. Insert chapter ten text here. Insert chapter ten text here. Insert chapter ten text here. Insert chapter ten text here. Insert chapter ten text here. Insert chapter ten text here.

APPENDIX-3

CURATED RESOURCES

"The Cure to Information Overload Is More Information."

– David Weinberger.

We live through the era of information overload, and it is humanly impossible to learn from all the knowledge and wisdom available. The reference resources that I have acknowledged in the chapters of this book are classics and authoritative sources. However, it is hard for readers to go through every one of those references in detail. The items curated in this section are impactful companions in your startup journey.

This section attempts to provide a set of resources with a short introduction to help first-time and even seasoned entrepreneurs to prioritize their reading plan. This is not an exhaustive list of excellent resources, as I haven't read nor examined every gem out there. I aim to keep the list manageable and select from what I have found helpful. I have not included any resource here that I have not gone through. I invite readers' feedback and recommendations on resources we must consider including in this curated list. This curated list will be available online with current updates on this book's website (bit.ly/notforedison.)

Books and White Papers

This section contains resources that will provide actionable help for founders depending on different aspects of scaling up firms.

1. *Giff Constable et al., "Talking to Humans: Success Starts with Understanding Your Customers," Giff Constable, 2014, ISBN 978-0-9908009-1-0.* Provides clear guidance to entrepreneurs on interviewing potential customers and effectively synthesizing the learning.
2. *Uday Phadke and Shailendra Vyakaranam, "The Scale-up Manual: Handbook of Innovators, Entrepreneurs, Teams and Firms," World Scientific Publishing Europe Ltd., 2019, ISBN 978-1-78634-5905.* A practitioner's reference, especially for deep-tech startup firms. This manual is a reference book with a rich set of tools that can be practically applied. It combines knowledge from different models and provides a data-driven framework for transforming technology innovation into a commercial business.
3. *Eric Ries, "The Lean Startup: How Constant Innovation Creates Radically Successful Businesses," Penguin UK, 2011, ISBN 978-0-670-92160-7*: The seminal book that explained the lean startup model, minimum viable product, etc., had a profound influence on the way internet-based software product development, adoption of agile methods in software engineering, etc.
4. *Steve Blank, "The Four Steps to the Epiphany: Successful Strategies for Products that Win," 5th Edition, John Wiley & Sons, 2020, ISBN 971-1-196-90351.* An excellent set of insights about how startups and larger companies are different and how to do customer development in detail. A must-read for first-time entrepreneurs, especially those starting with significant industry experience.
5. *Stefan H. Thomke, "Experimentation Works: The Surprising Power of Business Experiments," Harvard Business Review Press, 2020,*

ISBN 978-1-63369-710-2. Running disciplined business experiments is the only reliable way to design customer experience, develop products people buy, and innovate new business models. This is a well-researched resource for best practices in designing business experiments.

6. Ben Lamorte, *"The OKRs Field Book: A Step-by-Step Guide for Objectives and Key Results Coaches," Wiley, 2022, ISBN 978-1-119-81642-3*. An essential reference book for founders to deploy OKRs in their firms.

7. Josh Kaufman, *"The Personal MBA, Master the Art of Business" 10th Anniversary Edition, Portfolio/Penguin, Penguin Random House LLC, 2020, ISBN 978-1-59184-557-7*. An excellent reference book for new founders, especially functional specialists who want to develop a good foundation for managing their business.

8. Adrian Slywotzky, *"The Art of Profitability," Business Plus, 2003, ISBN 978-0-446-69227-4*. An amazingly easy-to-read book that packs many patterns for designing for profitability in business models. Another book by the same author, co-authored with *Karl Weber, "Demand: Creating What People Love Before They Know They Want It," Amazon Kindle Edition, 2011*, is also an excellent companion book.

9. Matt Blumberg, *"Startup CEO: A Field Guide to Scaling Up Your Business," Second Edition, John Wiley and Sons, 2020, ISBN 978-1-119-72366-0*. Most first-time entrepreneurs who have never done a CEO job before. Even for those who have performed a CEO or business unit head job in an established company, the change to being a founder/CEO of a startup is new. This book is a practical resource for founder/CEOs to develop perspectives and personally grow to perform the role well.

10. Matt Blumberg, *"Startup CXO: A Field Guide to Scaling Up Your Company's Critical Functions and Teams," John Wiley and Sons, 2021, ISBN 978-1-119-77257-6*. Most startup CXOs are in leadership roles of such complexity for the first time in their

careers. This book will help startup leaders scale themselves and their functions—an excellent reference book for all firms ambitious to scale up.
11. Alisa Cohn, *"From Start-up to Grown-up: Grow Your Leadership to Grow Your Business," Kogan Page Limited, 2022, 978-1-3986-0138-3*. Alisa Cohn is among the top startup coaches in the world. This book captures her wisdom and provides a treasure of coaching sessions with her if you are willing to read reflectively.
12. *Jim Clifton and Sangeeta Badal, "Born to Build: How to Build a Thriving Startup, A Winning Team, New Customers and Your Best Life Imaginable." Gallup Press, 2018, ISBN 978-1-59562-127-6*. Creating self-awareness is an essential key to the success of an entrepreneur. This book introduces the *Builder Profile* assessment that identifies innate talents and the types of entrepreneurial leaders. This book provides actionable guidelines to form and nurture effective, interdependent teams.
13. *Madhavan Ramanujam and Georg Tacke, "Monetizing Innovation: How Smart Companies Design the Product Around the Price," Wiley, 2016, ISBN 978-1-119-24086-0*. An excellent reference for startup founders and inventors who want to monetize intellectual property by bringing a product/service to the market.
14. V.K. *Saraswat, Neeraj Sinha, Naman Agrawal, Naba Suroor, Siddhey G. Shinde, "A New Lens for Innovation in New India—Introducing the Techno-commercial Readiness and Market Maturity Index, NITI Aayog, 2023, ISBN 978-81-956821-6-4*. This book is downloadable from https://niti.gov.in/sites/default/files/2023-07/TCRM-Matrix-Framework-FAD3.pdf (Last accessed 15-Jul-2023.) This book combines different maturity assessment frameworks for technology, commercial and market readiness to present a new way to assess the progress of an idea towards a viable business model.

15. *Geoff Ralston, "A Guide to Seed Fundraising," URL:* https://www.ycombinator.com/library/4A-a-guide-to-seed-fundraising *(Last accessed 15-Jul-2023.)* This web document is an excellent resource to help founders at the early stages of their technology venture think through their fundraising strategy ground up.

Websites/Blogs

1. Essays by Paul Graham (http://www.paulgraham.com/articles.html): a rich set of insightful articles about ideas, startups, and founder challenges. Very helpful for developing clarity about your startup ideas.
2. Customer Development Labs (https://customerdevlabs.com/start-here): Very focused and practical guidelines around customer development, a new skill for entrepreneurs to develop. This site provides several resources and linked websites that offer tips, tools, and education. The FOCUS framework (https://thefocusframework.com)
3. Stanford eCorner (https://ecorner.stanford.edu): eCorner creates content that helps entrepreneurs bring bold ideas to life and supports educators in developing thoughtful innovators.
4. Triple Chasm Company (https://www.thetriplechasm.com): Home for the Triple Chasm Model (TCM.) This site contains a rich set of resources and tools founders of science and technology-based ventures could use. The TCM is developed by working with thousands of deep technology ventures and publishes rigorous research findings at this site.
5. IdeaLab Lessons (https://25-lessons.idealab.com/introduction): IdeaLab is possibly the longest-running technology incubator in the world. This list

of 25 lessons about tech ventures.
6. Y Combinator (YC) Startup Library (https://www.ycombinator.com/library): YC is an early investor, and they have put together this library of materials, including the startup school for founders. The YC Startup School (SUS) is an excellent resource for new founders aspiring to establish their firms (https://www.startupschool.org.)
7. YNOS (https://www.ynos.in): A platform for the startup ecosystem in India. This platform connects startups, investors, experts, and intellectual property. Please check out the site for more details.
8. Van Vliet, V. (2010). Peter Drucker. Retrieved on 18-Jan-2022 from ToolsHero: https://www.toolshero.com/toolsheroes/peter-drucker/: This site contains a brief bio of Peter Drucker and a list of his famous quotes and publications. Those searching for the roots of management science would find several classics from Peter Drucker.
9. Society for Effectual Action (https://www.effectuation.org): This is the "go-to" site for learning about the current state of effectuation research and practice. It contains several resources for those interested in diving deeper into the details of effectuation.
10. Failory (https://www.failory.com/blog/seed-funding): A content site for startup founders that publishes weekly interviews and short and long-form articles to help founders. Specifically, the guide to raising seed funding is an excellent resource for knowing all early-stage fund-raising aspects.
11. Entrepreneurial Operating System (https://www.eosworldwide.com): This site presents a set of time-tested resources and tools relevant to firms that have achieved the initial business model fit and are aspiring to scale up or sustain an SME.

12. Andreessen Horowitz, or a16z (https://a16z.com): Silicon Valley venture capital firm founded in 2009. This site has a rich repository of content relevant to DeepTech founders.
13. Jerry Neumann invests in early-stage companies through Neu Venture Capital and teaches entrepreneurship at Columbia University. His blog, Reaction Wheel (https://reactionwheel.net), is rich in content in the context of DeepTech startups and profoundly explores the concept of uncertainty.
14. Shockwave Innovations (https://shockwaveinnovations.com): A rich set of resources and free courses for early-stage founders.

YouTube Videos, PODCASTS

This section compiles a few informative videos that founders will likely find helpful for reflection in the context of their firms.

1. **How to Start a Startup**, Lecture Series from Paul Graham, Sam Altman, Marc Andreessen, and other early Y Combinator founders and team (https://youtube.com/playlist?list=PL5q_lef6zVkaTY_cT1k7qFNF2TidHCe-1): This is a collection of twenty-one classes on the different aspects of building a startup, a complete masterclass. **Before the Startup with Paul Graham** (https://www.youtube.com/watch?v=f4_14pZlJBs) is a must-watch for first-time founders, ideally before starting their venture.
2. **Failure, Customer Discovery & Development** by Steve Blank, VC, UC Berkeley Professor (https://youtu.be/UkiHbRmKR4o): An insightful class on what startups are all about and the journey from idea to a business; bring out the big picture that startups are about searching for a business model.

3. **Launchpad Central Channel** (https://www.youtube.com/channel/UCAYx7tdUvd71Tz PaC7IOO6w/videos): This channel shares over 260 videos about the early stages of startup development (customer discovery, business model canvas, etc.)
4. **Tony Ulwick, Jobs to be done** (https://youtu.be/SoL1LxJeHBI, https://youtu.be/pUjkFL0kzBA, https://youtu.be/qQFUHapOJsQ): Detailed presentation from the expert on defining your market using the JTBD framework.
5. **Experiments to Find Product-Market Fit** (https://www.youtube.com/watch?v=AXvexQ0tZUQ) an online workshop by Justin Wilcox on Product Market Fit.
6. **David Riemer's series of videos on using storytelling** to communicate: https://venturewell.org/i-corps/llpvideos/david-riemer/: Venturewell, Retrieved on 01-Oct-2022.
7. **Pitch Your Idea: How to Get Buy-in from Investors**: Ash Maurya, Lenstack: (https://youtu.be/ukw6PfjAYWM): comprehensive training on how to think about your investor pitch and produce it.
8. **David Riemer on storytelling; story narrative and product narrative** (https://venturewell.org/i-corps/llpvideos/david-riemer): A set of short video talks that explain how to create the report for your firm's product and business.
9. **Something Ventured**: (https://vimeo.com/105745528): Directed by filmmakers Dan Geller and Dayna Goldfine, this documentary is brilliantly produced, capturing the origins of venture capital and the history of creating deep technology computer and software companies and the challenges of DeepTech founders, majorly set in the context of Silicon Valley, USA.

10. **Technological Revolutions and The Shape of Tomorrow**: (https://www.youtube.com/watch?v=TRUlHfPLnjE) Prof. Carlota Perez is an original thinker and contributor to a framework to help understand long-term technological transformations and their interaction with the economy, society, and the political system. In this talk, she explains the framework (May 2020.)
11. **Business Lessons You Can Learn from The Streets of India**, Capt. Raghu Raman, Josh Talks (https://youtu.be/12eD3K5Peu8): An inspiring talk about the street vendors in India and their business models.
12. **Becoming a 10x CEO**: (https://youtu.be/8plSShJj0a0) Mark Helow spent over 30 years studying, coaching, and learning from Entrepreneurs. He presents his observations in this short talk.

Reference Books

This section contains a list of reference books for those interested in diving deeper into entrepreneurship.

1. Everett M. Rogers, "Diffusion of Innovations," 5th Edition, Free Press, 2003, ISBN 978-0-743-22209-9. A classic work in innovation diffusion, first published in 1962. The book introduces several fundamental concepts of innovation adoption supported by research.
2. Clayton M. Christensen and Michael E. Raynor, "Innovator's Solution: Creating and Sustaining Successful Growth," Harvard Business Review Press, 2013, ISBN 978-1-422-19657-1. This book is a good reference for founders who have achieved at least product-market fit and are looking for rapid scale-up with greater predictability.
3. Uday Phadke, Shailendra Vyakarnam, "Camels, Tigers & Unicorns," World Scientific, 2018, ISBN 978-1-786-34322-

2. Result of decades-long research with early-stage technology ventures in different domains of DeepTech ventures. This book presents the Triple Chasm Model and associated components, frameworks, and tools.
4. Geoffrey A. Moore, "Crossing the Chasm: Marketing and Selling Disruptive Products to Mainstream Customers," 3rd Edition, Harper Business, 2014, ISBN 978-0-062-35394-8. Exciting reading about bringing cutting-edge technology products to the market with several stories focused on marketing.
5. Stuart Read, Saras Sarasvathy, Nick Dew, and Robert Wiltbank, "Effectual Entrepreneurship," 2nd edition, 2017, ISBN 978-1-315-68482-6. This book is a result of exploring entrepreneurs across industries, geographical locations, and time. It is written as a textbook on entrepreneurship and introduces the science of entrepreneurship—the common logic the authors observe in expert entrepreneurs across industries, geographic locations, and time. Indeed, an excellent reference for first-time entrepreneurs.
6. Robert D. Hisrich, Michael P. Peters, Dean A. Shepherd, and Sabyasachi Sinha, "Entrepreneurship," 11th Edition, 2020, McGraw Hill Education (India) Private Limited, ISBN 978-93-90113-30-9. This is an Indian edition of an internationally successful textbook on entrepreneurship. It is a rich textbook with systematic coverage of entrepreneurship topics over five major sections and several case studies—a handy reference for students, researchers, first-time entrepreneurs, and intrapreneurs.
7. Aswath Damodaran, "Applied Corporate Finance," 4th Edition, 2018, Wiley, ISBN 978-8-12657-302-8. An excellent corporate finance textbook for practitioners to understand the subject matter from the first principles.
8. Geoffrey West, "Scale: The Universal Laws of Life and Death in Organisms, Cities, and Companies," Weidenfeld & Nicolson, 2017, Amazon Kindle Edition. A thought-

provoking original book with systems thinking at its core explores interconnectedness in organisms and organizations.

9. Rajesh Jain, "Startup to Proficorn," Jaico Publishing House, ISBN 978-8-119-15308-4, 2023. An account of insights and experience by the entrepreneur in bootstrapping and growing multiple thriving firms out of their profits, and not taking any external venture capital.

10. Benjamin Graham and Jason Zweig, "The Intelligent Investor: The Definitive Book on Value Investing," Revised Edition, HarperCollins e-books (Amazon Kindle Edition,) 2009. Warren E. Buffett writes in the preface to the book's fourth edition in 1973, "I read the first edition of this book early in 1950 when I was nineteen. I thought then that it was by far the best book about investing ever written. I still think it is." (1)Learning value investing techniques is an excellent way to tame your mind to develop an investor mindset and work towards building a valuable firm. This book has been revised many times since it was written. You must also be willing not to consider the book as a manual or "how-to" book about economic value creation. Instead, if you look for gems of insights, you will discover a few that would change your perspectives forever. Be willing to adapt as needed.

11. Ethan Mollick, "The Unicorn's Shadow: Combating the Dangerous Myths that Hold back Startups, Founders, And Investors," Wharton School Press, 2020, ISBN 978-1-61363-097-6. Several functional perspectives for founders who are preparing to raise venture capital.

12. Nassim Nicholas Taleb, "Fooled by Randomness: The Hidden Role of Chance in Life and in the Markets," Penguin, Kindle Edition, ASIN: B002RI9BH6, 2007. This book presents perspectives on how we perceive luck, which would make you think deeply about the world and business. A word of caution about this book is that abstract in some

places and hard to comprehend. It is packed with wisdom that would make you reflect as you develop business strategy and realize the real meaning and impact of probability in life.

13. William Donaldson, "Simple Complexity: A Management Book For The Rest of Us: A Guide to Systems Thinking," Morgan James Publishing LLC, 2017, Amazon Kindle Edition. A practical, straightforward book to understand systems thinking in the context of smaller businesses.

REFERENCES

1. Warren Buffett's preface in the same book.

ABOUT THE AUTHOR

Sundara Nagarajan ("SN") passionately helps technologists develop and scale up their innovation-led firms to impact the world positively. He is the Managing Director of Innovation Scaleup Advisors (ISA), an enterprise development firm that helps technology-led companies grow globally. ISA serves startups, larger firms, and incubators, providing venture assistance, investors to assess ventures, and mature enterprises to adopt digital technologies to transform.

SN is an accomplished technologist with over three decades of experience in large global enterprises and early-stage firms, contributing to developing software system products. He has performed director-level technical leadership and executive management roles in product development and deployment, serving Customers worldwide at global technology majors, NetApp, HP, Philips, and Wipro. He founded a DeepTech firm, Bluefont. He also served in IPValue and IndusAge Partners.

SN serves the International Institute of Information Technology-Bangalore as Adjunct Faculty, a TiE Charter Member, a Senior Member of IEEE, a member of ACM, and a Gallup-certified Coach. SN holds an M.S. (by Research) degree from the Indian Institute of Technology Madras and a bachelor's degree in electrical engineering from the University of Calicut, being a topper from the University.

This book's website: *bit.ly/notforedison*

www.ingramcontent.com/pod-product-compliance
Lightning Source LLC
LaVergne TN
LVHW011416080426
835512LV00005B/86